MAR 2001

D
736
.L33
2000

EASTSI

Chicago Public Library

R0173682636

Leaders and generals.

P9-ASH-707

DISCARD

THE CHICAGO PUBLIC LIBRARY

CHICAGO PUBLIC LIBRARY
VODAK EAST SIDE BRANCH
3710 E. 106TH STREET
CHICAGO, IL 60617

AMERICAN
WAR LIBRARY

★ ★ ★ ★

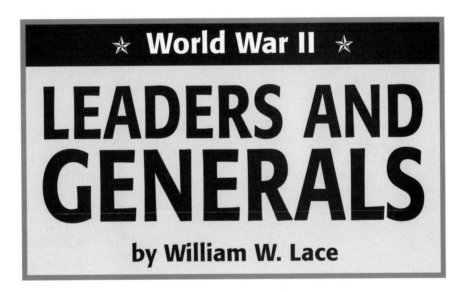

★ World War II ★

# LEADERS AND GENERALS

by William W. Lace

Lucent Books, P.O. Box 289011, San Diego, CA 92198-9011

Titles in The American War Library series include:

**World War II**
Hitler and the Nazis
Kamikazes
Leaders and Generals
Life as a POW
Life of an American Soldier in
  Europe
Strategic Battles in Europe
Strategic Battles in the Pacific
The War at Home
Weapons of War

**The Civil War**
Leaders of the North and South
Life Among the Soldiers and
  Cavalry
Lincoln and the Abolition of
  Slavery
Strategic Battles
Weapons of War

Library of Congress Cataloging-in-Publication Data

Lace, William W.
      Leaders and generals of World War II  /  by William W. Lace.
         p.    cm.—(American war library)
      Includes bibliographical references (p.   ) and index.
      Summary: Chronicles the lives and careers of eight military
leaders who served during World War II, including Rommel, Zhukov,
Yamamoto, Nimitz, Eisenhower, Von Manstein, Montgomery, and
MacArthur.
      ISBN 1-56006-664-4  (lib. : alk. paper)
      1. World War, 1939–1945—Biography Juvenile literature.
2. Generals—Biography Juvenile literature. 3. Military biography
Juvenile literature. [1. Generals. 2. Military biography. 3. World
War, 1939–1945.] I. Title. II. Series: American war library series.
D736.L33   2000
940.54'0092'2—dc21
[B]                                                                          99-33487
                                                                                CIP

Copyright 2000 by Lucent Books, Inc.
P.O. Box 289011, San Diego, California 92198-9011

No part of this book may be reproduced or used in any other form or by
any other means, electrical, mechanical, or otherwise, including, but not
limited to, photocopy, recording, or any information storage and re-
trieval system, without prior written permission from the publisher.

Printed in the U.S.A.

EAS

# ☆ Contents ☆

Vodak / East Side Branch
10542 S. Ewing Ave.
Chicago, IL 60617

# A Nation Forged by War

The United States, like many nations, was forged and defined by war. Despite Benjamin Franklin's opinion that "There never was a good war or a bad peace," the United States owes its very existence to the War of Independence, one to which Franklin wholeheartedly subscribed. The country forged by war in 1776 was tempered and made stronger by the Civil War in the 1860s.

The Texas Revolution, the Mexican-American War, and the Spanish-American War expanded the country's borders and gave it overseas possessions. These wars made the United States a world power, but this status came with a price, as the nation became a key but reluctant player in both World War I and World War II.

Each successive war further defined the country's role on the world stage. Following World War II, U.S. foreign policy redefined itself to focus on the role of defender, not only of the freedom of its own citizens, but also of the freedom of people everywhere. During the cold war that followed World War II until the collapse of the Soviet Union, defending the world meant fighting communism. This goal, manifested in the Korean and Vietnam conflicts, proved elusive, and soured the American public on its achievability. As the United States emerged as the world's sole superpower, American foreign policy has been guided less by national interest and more on protecting international human rights. But as involvement in Somalia and Kosovo prove, this goal has been equally elusive.

As a result, the country's view of itself changed. Bolstered by victories in World Wars I and II, Americans first relished the role of protector. But, as war followed war in a seemingly endless procession, Americans began to doubt their leaders, their motives, and themselves. The Vietnam War especially caused people to question the validity of sending its young people to die in places where they were not particularly wanted and for people who did not seem especially grateful.

While the most obvious changes brought about by America's wars have been geopolitical in nature, many other aspects of society have been touched. War often does not bring about change directly, but acts instead like the catalyst in a chemical reaction, accelerating changes already in progress.

Some of these changes have been societal. The role of women in the United States had been slowly changing, but World War II put thousands into the workforce and into uniform. They might have gone back to being housewives after the war, but equality, once experienced, would not be forgotten.

Likewise, wars have accelerated technological change. The necessity for faster airplanes and a more destructive bomb led to the development of jet planes and nuclear energy. Artificial fibers developed for parachutes in the 1940s were used in the clothing of the 1950s.

Lucent Books' American War Library covers key wars in the development of the nation. Each war is covered in several volumes, to allow for more detail, context, and to provide volumes on often neglected subjects, such as the kamikazes of World War II, or weapons used in the Civil War. As with all Lucent Books, notes, annotated bibliographies, and appendixes such as glossaries give students a launching point for further research. In addition, sidebars and archival photographs enhance the text. Together, each volume in The American War Library will aid students in understanding how America's wars have shaped and changed its politics, economics, and society.

# The Great Man Theory

**H**istorians and philosophers have argued for millennia over the question of whether individuals shape events or are shaped by them. The notion that history results from the ideas and deeds of individuals is sometimes called the Great Man theory. It dates from the writings of Plutarch in ancient Greece and was continued by writers such as Thomas Carlyle in Scotland.

It is tempting to accept such a view. After all, could there have been Christianity without Jesus of Nazareth? Would Hellenistic culture have spread without Alexander the Great to carry it? Did the single-minded determination of one man, William the Conqueror, decide the subsequent history of England? Would polio still be a killer or crippler of thousands had it not been for Jonas Salk?

The opposite view is taken by such philosophers as Germany's Wilhelm Friedrich Hegel. Hegelianism teaches that history is a progression of human thought and spirit along a logical path leading to freedom and self-understanding. To Hegel, individuals are only players of brief roles in an ongoing drama.

*Alexander the Great (left), William the Conqueror*

*Wilhelm Friedrich Hegel disagreed with the Great Man theory, believing that significant events are destined to happen when their time in history comes.*

The Hegelist, then, would argue that Jesus' teachings would have evolved naturally even if Jesus had never lived, and that someone would eventually have spread the essentials of what developed as Hellenistic culture, taken England into the European

orbit, or invented a polio vaccine. In other words, events happen when their time in history comes.

As is common with philosophical opposites, the reality is probably somewhere in between. Events that dramatically impact history occur when opportunity meets ability. The teachings of Jesus were not completely new. They were an outgrowth, an extension of Judaic thought that had been evolving since Old Testament times. Yet, it took someone with Jesus' force of personality and—Christians say—divine inspiration to articulate the new creed.

World War II is also a mix of history and the individual. While the war's seeds were definitely sown after World War I, Adolf Hitler exploited Germans' dissatisfaction and poverty to launch a movement to gain world dominance. Truly, the war itself changed the world, and the leaders in that war made a pivotal impact on the future of the world.

The eight men whose lives and careers are detailed in this book helped to form the events that shaped the world for the rest of the century. The fates of nations hung on their abilities, their daring and genius, their faults and frailties. As much as is possible for individuals, they *made* history.

# Chapter 1

# Rommel: "Desert Fox"

rwin Rommel, his soldiers said, had *Fingerspitzengefühl,* a "feeling in the fingers," when engaged in battle. His senses seemed to stretch forth wherever he fought, especially in the desert of North Africa. "I sniff through the country like a fox,"[1] he was fond of saying. Thus he was known by friend and foe as the Desert Fox.

Since he acted largely from intuition, Rommel's actions were often unpredictable. "Certainly Rommel should not have dared attack us as soon as he did,"[2] complained a British general. He also did not always follow orders. Even though the British had broken Germany's code and frequently knew what Rommel's orders were from Berlin, he so often disobeyed orders that the information could not be trusted.

Unlike many German generals, Rommel was not the product of a family military tradition. He was born in 1891, the son and grandson of schoolmasters. The only military experience in his family background was his father's brief time as an artillery lieutenant.

Known for his toughness later in life, Rommel was anything but tough as a child. He was small for his age, with hair so blond and skin so pale that other children nicknamed him White Bear. His sister Helena later described him as being gentle and docile.

At school he showed signs of intelligence but was too lazy to study and had little interest in any of his subjects. When challenged, he could excel, but he seldom put forth the necessary effort.

Rommel seemed to come to life as a teenager. His grades improved, especially in mathematics—his father's specialty—and he became an enthusiastic bicyclist and skier. He also became interested in aircraft and made plans to seek a university degree in engineering.

His father, perhaps influenced by Rommel's earlier school performance, discouraged his plans and advised him on an army

*In combat, Erwin Rommel often disobeyed orders from his superiors, preferring to follow his intuition instead.*

## Training and Marriage

According to the custom of the time, Rommel entered the regiment as a private and was promoted to corporal, then to sergeant. He was sent to officer training school at Danzig and there met and fell in love with Lucie Mollin, the cousin of a fellow cadet. They would be married four years later.

In 1912 Rommel passed his examinations with scores barely above average and was commissioned a lieutenant. Two years later, on the outbreak of World War I, his regiment was sent to Belgium. On August 21, 1914, he saw his first action, one that gave a good indication of his ability and daring. On patrol with three other men, he spotted about twenty French soldiers taking a coffee break. Rather than fall back and get more troops, he led his men in an all-out charge, yelling and firing their rifles as they ran. Ten of the Frenchmen were killed and the rest taken prisoner.

The sudden headlong charge, taking an enemy by surprise, would become a Rommel hallmark. His philosophy was one of hitting first and hitting hard. He later wrote, "The day goes to the side that first plasters its opponents with fire."[3]

That summer, after recovering from a leg wound, Rommel was promoted to full

career. The eighteen-year-old Rommel obeyed and in the spring of 1910 was accepted by the 124th Württemberg Regiment.

lieutenant and posted to a mountain battalion on the southern border of Austria. In October 1917 he led a small force in the capture of Mount Matajur, taking more than nine thousand prisoners and suffering only six dead and thirty wounded. This exploit earned him a promotion to captain. Shortly afterward, after leading the capture of the village of Longarone, he was awarded the Pour le Mérite, a decoration normally reserved for senior officers.

By now, Rommel had completed a transformation from lazy child to an ideal military officer. He was a stern disciplinarian but had a sense of humor and was admired and even loved by the soldiers who served under him. He became an ardent student of military affairs and wrote a much-respected book on infantry tactics. He had virtually no interests outside the army, reading little except for military history and taking no notice of literature, art, or music. He did not smoke and drank only a glass or two of wine at the most, something that set him apart from his fellow officers.

## After the War

Rommel was one of the relatively few officers who remained in the stripped-down German army after World War I. Rommel commanded an infantry company and then a machine gun company. He qualified as a military ski instructor. He learned everything he could about tanks and became an expert mechanic. He also served as an instructor at an infantry school. He tried to learn everything he could about anything dealing with the army.

In 1933, after eight long years as a captain, he was promoted to major and took command of an infantry battalion stationed

*In a photograph taken during World War I, Rommel wears the Pour le Mérite (hanging from collar).*

in the city of Goslar. It was there, in 1934, that he first met Adolf Hitler, leader of the Nazi Party who had become chancellor of Germany in 1933. Hitler reviewed the battalion and congratulated Rommel on his Pour le Mérite.

Whether Hitler remembered the young officer is not known, but two years later Rommel was put in charge of security at the giant Nazi rally at Nuremberg, and in 1938, newly promoted to colonel, he was ordered to command the battalion that would escort Hitler on his triumphal entry into Prague, Czechoslovakia, after that country was occupied by Germany.

Hitler, himself of a middle-class background, felt at home with the blunt, forthright Rommel, much preferring him to members of the aristocracy. When World War II erupted in September 1939, Rommel was promoted to major general and given command of Hitler's headquarters battalion. He now accompanied the Nazi leader virtually everywhere, including the battlefields of Poland, where he carefully noted the importance of tanks.

Finally, Rommel worked up enough courage to ask Hitler to be transferred to a combat command. "What do you want?" Hitler asked, and Rommel replied, "Command of a Panzer [tank] division."[4] Hitler

*Like Rommel, Hitler had a middle-class background and felt at ease with the general. In September 1939, Rommel was given command of Hitler's headquarters battalion.*

agreed, and in February 1940 Rommel was made commander of the Seventh Panzer Division. He left with Hitler's thanks and an autographed copy of the dictator's autobiography *Mein Kampf* (*My Struggle*).

## The Ghost Division

With the invasion of Belgium and France in May 1940, Rommel was in his element once again. He pushed his division hard, with no pause for meals or sleep. He popped up where the French least expected. Even the German headquarters couldn't keep up with the Seventh Division's whereabouts and it became known as the *Gespenterdivision*, or Ghost Division. He continued his advance, not stopping until he reached the city of Cherbourg on the English Channel.

For his exploits, Rommel was awarded the Knight's Cross, the highest form of the Iron Cross. Hitler paid him a personal visit.

Joseph Goebbels, Hitler's minister of propaganda, used newsreels to make Rommel something of a national hero.

In September 1940 the British, along with their allies from Australia and New Zealand, had fought off an Italian drive toward Egypt and had driven the Italians back five hundred miles to Tripoli. Hitler was afraid that an Italian defeat would cause Benito Mussolini's government to fall. He decided to send German troops to help his

*In the French countryside, Rommel (center) and his staff plan their next move. His troops became known as the Ghost Division due to Rommel's stealthy tactics.*

ally. He needed a strong, energetic commander, and Rommel was his man.

In February 1941 Hitler ordered the Fifth Light Division and the Fifteenth Panzer Division to Tripoli as the Deutsches Afrika Korps with Rommel as commander. Technically, Rommel was under the command of an Italian general, but he had the right to appeal to Berlin if he thought the Italians' orders placed German troops in unwarranted danger.

## Ignoring Hitler's Order

Rommel was a traditional soldier with respect for the traditional rules of war. This included the humane treatment of prisoners.

In October 1942 Adolf Hitler sent out a directive saying, "All enemies on so-called Commando missions in Europe or Africa challenged by German troops, even if they are to all appearances soldiers in uniform, whether armed or unarmed, in battle or in flight, are to be slaughtered to the last man."

General Siegfried Westphal, who served under Rommel when the order was given, testified years later at the Allied war crimes trials in Nuremberg as to how it was received. The quotation is from *Rommel, the Desert Fox* by Desmond Young:

Marshal Rommel and I read it [the order] standing beside our truck. I then immediately proposed that we should not publish it. We burnt it at once, where we stood. . . . We did not wish this message to reach our troops, for that would have led to an aggravation of the war of which it would have been impossible to foresee the consequences. That was why the message was burnt ten minutes after it was received.

Rommel's first task was to keep the British from taking Tripoli. The conservative Italians wanted him to establish a defensive position, but he promptly ignored his orders and began an eastward push. The first clash of German-Italian and Allied troops came on March 31 at Mersa Brega. After putting up stiff resistance at first, the British began to fall back. As Rommel later wrote, "It was a chance I could not resist."[5] Despite Italian protests, he ordered a full-scale offensive.

It was like France all over again. Rommel's troops overran the exhausted British, covering more than fifty miles each day. Rommel, a skilled pilot, used a small plane to survey the advance. At one point, seeing a column of tanks he thought moved too slowly, he swooped down and dropped a message reading: "If you do not move at once, I shall come down! Rommel."[6]

### Invasion of Egypt

The British fell back to the city of Tobruk, which their high command ordered to be held at all cost. Rommel surrounded the heavily fortified city on April 10 but was unable to take it. Leaving some of his forces, he resumed the advance and by April 24 had crossed the border into Egypt, capturing the important mountain pass at Halfaya.

In six weeks Rommel had regained all that the British had gained in four months. Neither the British nor the German high command, which had reluctantly endorsed his offensive when it was well under way,

One of Rommel's panzers tears through the desert. From Tripoli, the Afrika Korps chased the British into Egypt at the speed of fifty miles per day.

knew what to make of this impetuous general. Chief of Staff Franz Halder complained that he "had not sent in a single clear report."[7]

Rommel was convinced that with additional troops, tanks, and supplies, he could drive the British out of Egypt. He flew to Berlin to plead his case but was given only vague assurances of support. To Hitler and the German general staff, busy planning an invasion of the Soviet Union, the war in North Africa was a sideshow.

To the British, however, it was much more. They poured reinforcements into Egypt and in mid-June launched Operation Battleaxe to try again to dislodge Rommel

from Halfaya Pass. Again, they failed. A frustrated British prime minister Winston Churchill replaced the British commander, General Archibald Wavell, with General Claude Auchinleck, commander in chief in India.

Auchinleck sought to dispel the growing notion among his subordinates that Rommel's abilities bordered on the superhuman. He told his men that they were to henceforth refer to the enemy as "Germany," "the Axis powers," or simply "the enemy," not "Rommel."

Nevertheless, the British went to extraordinary lengths to try to remove Rommel from the scene. In November 1941 commandos led by Colonel Geoffrey Keyes landed on the Libyan coast by submarine. One of their goals was the assassination of Rommel. They succeeded in reaching his house, but those inside had been alerted by a noise and a gun battle broke out during which Keyes was killed. As it turned out, Rommel had been in Rome celebrating his birthday with Lucie and their son, Manfred.

## Operation Crusader

Auchinleck launched his offensive, Operation Crusader, soon afterward. One British column attacked the Halfaya Pass while others swung around toward Tobruk with the intent of linking up with the forces inside the besieged city. The battle raged back and forth over a wide area and became so confused that at one point Rommel walked into a New Zealand field hospital thinking it was German, while the doctor in charge thought he was a Polish officer. Rommel realized his mistake and quickly left before he could be captured.

The battle was fought on even terms, but Rommel had expended far too much time and energy in a failed thrust intended to trap the British. He had to fall back to Tobruk and begin a retreat that by January 10, 1942, took him all the way back to El Agheila, where he had been the previous March.

This time, however, it was the British who had overextended themselves. Sensing this, Rommel launched a counterattack on January 21 and by February 6 had pushed the British back three hundred miles to Gazala just west of Tobruk. After four months of skirmishing, Rommel attacked on June 11 and the British had to fall back toward Egypt.

Rommel then unleashed a furious land and air attack. On June 21 Tobruk fell to the Germans. It was Rommel's largest victory, and Hitler rewarded him by making him, at age forty-nine, the youngest field marshal in the German army. For the British, however, the fall of Tobruk was considered as great a defeat as the fall of France. Churchill had to survive a vote in the British Parliament that could have led to his removal as prime minister.

Rommel was now confident he could successfully invade Egypt. Mussolini was so sure of success that he came to Africa prepared to ride into Cairo, the Egyptian capital, in triumph. Rommel advanced swiftly, crossing into Egypt via the Halfaya Pass and onward another 250 miles to El Alamein, only seventy-five miles from the Nile River, but he had come too far, too fast. In a battle that raged throughout July, Auchinleck's defensive line held and he was able to counterattack.

The German advance was halted, and a disappointed Mussolini had to return to Rome. Churchill wanted Auchinleck to press his advantage and attack, but the British commander was cautious. Impatient,

*A victorious Rommel chats with comrades after recapturing Tobruk. For his triumph, Hitler promoted Rommel to the rank of field marshal.*

Churchill replaced Auchinleck with General Harold Alexander as commander in chief. The command of the Eighth Army went to General Bernard Montgomery.

## Second El Alamein

Yet, it wasn't until October 23, when Rommel was in Germany recovering from an illness, that the British generals launched the attack that began the Second Battle of El Alamein. Rommel hurried back to the front and counterattacked, but was driven back by massive artillery bombardment and air attacks.

Hitler sent a message ordering Rommel to fight to the last man. Rommel ignored him and began a slow retreat to the west during which he showed skills just as considerable as those he displayed while advancing. By mid-January 1943 the Germans had retreated more than a thousand miles to Tunisia.

On March 9 Rommel flew to Rome and then to Hitler's headquarters in the Soviet Union, pleading for reinforcements. By this time, however, he was very ill and Hitler had little confidence in either his health or his abilities. He was relieved of his command and never returned to Africa.

After a long convalescence and a series of routine assignments, Rommel was assigned in November 1943 to inspect German defenses along the French coast and to make recommendations on how to best withstand the expected Allied invasion. Most of his recommendations were ignored by Hitler, and the successful invasion of France took place on June 6.

Meanwhile, Rommel's time back in Europe had convinced him that Germany could not win the war. While he never went so far as to advocate Hitler's assassination, he agreed with an increasing number of military and government leaders who thought that the Nazi leader should be removed from power so that Germany would be spared a disastrous invasion that would destroy much of the country.

On July 20 an attempt on Hitler's life failed. The investigation revealed that Rommel had been involved with some of the conspirators. Hitler determined that Rommel must die, but he did not want the German people to know that the man regarded as a hero had opposed him.

## Rommel and the Nazis

Rommel was a soldier. Nothing much outside the military interested him. Once, shown what another officer called a beautiful view, he began describing how he would position troops. His disinterest extended to politics. While he could not have been totally unaware of the Nazi Party doctrine on race, particularly as it applied to Jews, he had no idea how much it dominated Adolf Hitler's thinking.

Early in 1943, on one of his trips to Germany from North Africa, Rommel was at a gathering that included Hitler and some of the top Nazis. Rommel, naively unaware of the mass murders of the Jews taking place in Poland, suggested that since Germany's official policy toward the Jews was creating a bad image abroad, Hitler should appoint a Jewish *Gauleiter*, or Nazi district leader.

There was a stunned silence. Then, as quoted in *Knight's Cross* by David Fraser, Hitler said, "You've understood nothing of what I want." Later, after Rommel had left the room, Hitler said to his cronies, "Doesn't he realize the Jews are the cause of the war?"

## Trial or Suicide?

On October 15 Rommel was visited by two generals sent by Hitler. They gave him a choice, either face a public trial or commit suicide. If Rommel chose suicide, he would be buried with full military honors instead of being denounced as a traitor. His family would be unharmed, and his estate would remain intact.

Rommel left his visitors waiting while he went upstairs and told Lucie the news. Then he said good-bye to Manfred, now fifteen years old. He left the house moments later, holding his field marshal's baton, and got into a waiting car with the two generals. The car was driven to a secluded area where Rommel was given a small bottle of cyanide. A half hour later, Lucie received a call telling her that her husband was dead of a "heart attack."

Rommel was one of the great field commanders of World War II. In circum-

*Hitler shows Mussolini the room in which a bomb failed to kill the Nazi leader on July 20. Rommel had been involved with some of the conspirators and paid for this with his life.*

His superiors saw him as a complainer, constantly pleading for more men, more planes, more tanks. This was undoubtedly true, but only because the lack of men and supplies was very real. With Hitler occupied with the Soviet Union, Rommel never received the support given his enemies. Had he received such support, the outcome of the North African campaign might have been very different.

One of his greatest enemies, Auchinleck, wrote, "If there ever was a general whose sole preoccupation was the destruction of the enemy, it was he. He showed no mercy and expected none."[8] And General Fritz Bayerlein wrote that a soldier's merit can be measured by

stances that would have resulted in the surrender of lesser leaders, he not only held his own, but repeatedly struck back with such fury that imminent defeat turned into victory. While some experts argue that he was too rash and that his very boldness may have led to his final defeat, that defeat would probably have come much sooner had it not been for his uncanny feel for the battlefield and his willingness to drive both his soldiers and himself.

physical capacity, intelligence, mobility, nerve, pugnacity, daring and stoicism. A commander of men requires these qualities in even greater measure and in addition must be outstanding in his toughness, devotion to his men, instinctive judgement of terrain and enemy, speed of reaction and spirit. In General Rommel these qualities were embodied in rare degree and I have known no other officer in whom they were so combined.[9]

# Chapter 2

# Zhukov: Soviet Hero

**W**henever and wherever he faced a crisis during World War II—Leningrad, Moscow, Stalingrad, Kursk—Soviet leader Joseph Stalin called on the same general, Georgi Zhukov. When the time came for the conquest of Berlin, Stalin chose Zhukov to lead it. "Zhukov is my George B. McClellan [one of Abraham Lincoln's generals during the Civil War]," the Soviet dictator said. "Like McClellan, he always wants more men, more cannon, more guns. Also more planes. He never has enough. But Zhukov has never lost a battle."[10]

Zhukov's style, indeed, was to amass as large a force as possible, wait for his enemies to wear themselves out, then hit as hard and fast as he could. He was often as ruthless with his own troops as with the enemy, willing to suffer huge losses if it meant victory. "If we come to a mine field, our infantry attack exactly as if it were not there,"[11] he once boasted.

He was respected by those who served

under him, but not loved. He demanded swift results and would bully his officers, threatening them with demotion and even a firing squad if they failed to perform. "If you don't know how, we'll teach you," he would tell his troops. "If you don't want to, we'll make you."[12] Even one of his closest friends, General Konstantin Rokossovsky, admitted that "sometimes his severity exceeded permissible limits."[13]

If Zhukov was harsh, it was because the times demanded it. After the surprise attack by Germany in June 1941, the Soviet Union was on the verge of defeat. Its survival depended on extraordinary heroism and unbelievable suffering and hardship on the part of both soldiers and citizens. Had Zhukov not been a hard taskmaster, the war might have been lost.

Zhukov came from the humblest of beginnings, born on November 19, 1896, the son of a poor shoemaker in a village southwest of Moscow. The family's house, he wrote, was "a tumble-down affair, one corner of which had sunk deep in the ground, and the outer walls and roof were overgrown with moss and grass."[14]

## Hard at Work

When he was six, Zhukov began to help support his family, catching fish in nearby streams and trading them to other villagers for soup and meat. At age seven he went to work in the hay meadows, badly blistering his hands on the pitchfork handle and accidentally slicing off the little finger of his left hand with a sickle.

In the fall of 1903, he began lessons at the parish school and quickly showed exceptional ability. At the same time, he began to become aware of discontent among the Russian peasantry. Strangers began to appear in village taverns telling stories of repression and urging the peasants to rise up against their landlords and the nobility.

Zhukov finished school in 1906 at the top of his class, but his family could not afford any additional education, so he was apprenticed to his uncle, a furrier in Moscow, attending school at night and studying by the light of a single dim lightbulb in a bathroom.

He finished his apprenticeship in 1911 and stayed on with his uncle as a craftsman, moving out of the rooms where the apprentices lived into lodgings of his own. He fell in love with his landlady's daughter, and the couple made tentative plans to marry.

Zhukov's career, studies, and romance all were interrupted, however, by World War I, and he

*Georgi Zhukov never lost a battle. He was willing to accept massive casualties in combat if victory were the result.*

was drafted into the army in August 1915 and assigned to a cavalry unit. As a country boy, he had learned to ride, but riding while wielding a saber or a lance was hard work. Soon, as with the pitchfork years earlier, his hands were covered with blisters.

He worked hard, however, and soon was chosen for training as a noncommissioned officer. Part of his training was to view the soldiers under him with little human feeling and to treat them accordingly. He was to demonstrate such ruthlessness as a general in World War II.

*Armed with sabers, a Russian cavalry unit charges into action during World War I. For his service in the cavalry, Zhukov was selected for training as a noncommissioned officer.*

## War and Revolution

When the training was completed, Zhukov was assigned to a cavalry division fighting the Germans near Kharkov. Two months later he was thrown from his horse by an exploding mine and suffered a severe concussion. Before he could return to active duty, Russia was out of the war and in the midst of a bloody revolution.

Weary of war and of centuries of exploitation, the Russian people at last rose up in rebellion. The monarchy was overthrown, and several factions battled for power. Zhukov aligned himself with the Bolshevik, or Communist, faction, joining the Red Army in 1918 and the Communist Party in 1919. He fought bravely in the civil war and was severely wounded by a hand grenade.

It took two months for Zhukov to recover, but his bravery and ability had caught the attention of his superiors and he was sent to a class for future commanders. He completed the course and was commissioned an officer in 1920.

During the 1920s he commanded a cavalry regiment but had taken an interest in tanks. When two tank regiments were created, Stalin chose Zhukov to command one of them. In rapid succession he was promoted to brigade commander and division commander, performing so well that he was awarded the Order of Lenin.

Stalin eventually was persuaded, however, that tanks should not operate independently and should take the secondary role of protecting ground troops. Zhukov's tank regiment was disbanded over his strong objections. Eventually, when German tank forces overran the Soviet army in 1941,

Stalin would order Dimitri Pavlov, the man who convinced him to abandon tank regiments, to be shot.

## Victory in Mongolia

Zhukov continued his spectacular rise within the Red Army, and in 1939, now commanding a cavalry corps, he was ordered to Mongolia, which had been invaded by Japanese troops. In August, along the Khalkin-Gol River, he won a battle in which the Japanese lost fifty thousand men to the Soviets' ten thousand and were pushed out of Mongolia. When the forty-three-year-old Zhukov returned to Moscow, he was personally congratulated by Stalin, promoted to general, and awarded the title Hero of the Soviet Union.

*Soldiers killed during the Russian civil war await burial. Zhukov's bravery and skill during the conflict eventually earned him an officer's commission.*

Zhukov's good fortune was due to two factors. First, Stalin had taken a personal interest in him. Second, thanks to Stalin, there was plenty of room at the top of the Soviet military ranks. As part of an attempt to eliminate any threat to his power, Stalin in

## A Hard Taskmaster

Zhukov was widely known as a tough commander, one who demanded instant obedience, supreme effort, and complete results from those who served under him. This was evident as early as 1939, when he commanded a regiment against the Japanese in Mongolia. This recollection by one of his officers is quoted in *Zhukov* by Otto Preston Chaney:

> Zhukov ordered one of his divisions to attack the Japanese fortifications. The outcome of the entire operation depended on the success of this assault. The division was beaten off with heavy losses and found itself pinned to the ground. . . . A short time later Zhukov himself summoned the division commander to the telephone. Upon finding that he had not yet managed to start the division moving, Zhukov asked: "Will you be able to start the attack?" The division commander cautiously expressed doubt. Then Zhukov said: "I hereby relieve you of command of the division. Hand the receiver over to your Chief of Staff." Zhukov put the same question to the latter. The Chief of Staff answered in the affirmative. . . . But the Chief of Staff did not succeed in launching a new attack either. When he reported this fact to Zhukov, he received the same order: "I relieve you of command of the division. Wait for the arrival of a new division commander." Zhukov sent a new commander from his own staff . . . and the attack succeeded.

1937–1938 had imprisoned or executed 403 of the top 706 army officers. Of the 20 senior officers in 1937, only 4 survived.

The lack of leadership in the Red Army was demonstrated in the winter of 1939–40 when it invaded tiny Finland. A campaign that was supposed to take a few weeks lasted four months and cost many lives. Stalin decided to reorganize the army. In January 1941 Zhukov, whose troops had just successfully played the part of German invaders in practice maneuvers, was among the top officers summoned by Stalin to a meeting. Stalin called on the chief of staff, General Kirill Meretskov, to explain why the "defenders" had been defeated. Flustered, Meretskov could not give a satisfactory answer. Stalin broke in: "Comrade Timoshenko [the commissar of defense] has requested that Comrade Zhukov be named Chief of the General Staff. Do you all agree?"[15] As frequently happened when Stalin spoke, there was no disagreement.

By this time World War II was well under way. When Germany invaded Poland in 1939, the Soviets, according to a secret deal with the Germans, had moved in and "liberated" the eastern half of the country. German troops had overrun France but were unsuccessful in forcing Great Britain to surrender. Nazi chief Adolf Hitler then turned eastward and prepared for a surprise invasion of the Soviet Union.

## Stalin's Suspicion

The Soviets should not have been at all surprised. German forces had been massed on

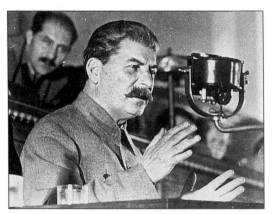

*After being betrayed by the Nazis, Joseph Stalin (pictured) ordered Zhukov to defend the cities of Kiev, Smolensk, and Leningrad against invading German troops.*

the border. British prime minister Winston Churchill sent Stalin word that his intelligence agents had discovered German plans to attack. Stalin refused to believe that Hitler would violate the nonaggression pact signed in 1939. Ever suspicious, Stalin thought Churchill was trying to trick him into entering the war.

Senior army officers believed the attack was imminent but were afraid to press the point with Stalin. Zhukov was among them. Later he said, "I do not disclaim responsibility for the fact that perhaps I did not prove to Stalin in a sufficiently convincing manner the necessity of bringing our Army to combat readiness. Possibly, I did not have enough influence with him for this."[16]

Zhukov was first sent south to Kiev in the Ukraine to organize defenses in that area. The Germans advanced rapidly, but Zhukov's troops were able to stop them at Smolensk and the invasion slowed down. Meanwhile, however, Hitler had ordered his troops to take Leningrad in the north and burn it to the ground. As the German noose tightened around the city in September, Stalin relieved the commander there and ordered Zhukov to take over.

Zhukov immediately took the order a step farther. He told the defenders that they would face a firing squad if they failed. He organized citizens into round-the-clock work crews, writing later that "dying of hunger at their jobs, in the streets, and in their unheated apartments, the working people of Leningrad gave no thought to themselves."[17] The German advance slowed, and when it did, Zhukov went on the offensive. Little ground was gained, but the city was out of immediate danger.

## The Threat to Moscow

Zhukov was desperately needed elsewhere. On October 7 he was ordered to Moscow by Stalin, who told him that Soviet armies to the west of the city were retreating. The Germans were only sixty miles from Moscow. Zhukov hurried to the front to assess the situation. He was still there when a telegram arrived from Stalin. It read, "The Supreme Commander in Chief [Stalin] orders you to go to the headquarters of the Western [army group]."[18]

Just as he had in Leningrad, Zhukov organized the Soviet forces defending Moscow. When the troops near Vyaz'ma were surrounded, rather than surrender

## The Battle of Moscow

When German troops threatened to capture Moscow in the winter of 1941, Stalin sent for Zhukov, who masterminded the defense of the city and planned the counterattack that removed the threat to the Soviet capital. In *Zhukov's Greatest Battles*, excerpted from his memoirs, he gave this rather self-serving impression of the importance of the victory:

> For the first time in six months of war, in the Battle of Moscow the Red Army inflicted a major defeat on the main forces of the enemy. It was the first strategic victory over the *Wehrmacht* [German army] since the beginning of World War II. Even before the Battle of Moscow, the Soviet armed forces had conducted a number of important operations that slowed the advance of the *Wehrmacht* . . . but none of those operations was equal in scale or results to the great battle before the walls of the Soviet capital. The skilled conduct of defensive operations, the successful launching of counterattacks and the swift transition to a counteroffensive greatly enriched Soviet military art and demonstrated the growing strategic and operational-tactical maturity of Soviet military commanders. . . . After the defeat of the Germans before Moscow, the strategic initiative on all sectors of the Soviet-German front passed to the Soviet command.

they fought until annihilated and bought precious time for the rest of the army to pull back to a new front. When that front had to be abandoned, Zhukov sent a message to all forces under his command:

Comrades! In this grave hour of danger for our state, the life of each soldier belongs to the Fatherland. The homeland demands from each one of you the greatest effort, courage, heroism and steadfastness. The homeland calls on us to stand like an indestructible wall and to bar the Fascist hordes from our beloved Moscow. What we require now, as never before, are vigilance, iron discipline, organization, determined action, unbending will for victory and a readiness for self-sacrifice.[19]

His troops responded. The civilians did their part. More than 450,000 people, most of them women, turned out in the snow to construct tank barricades. The German advance continued; they got within fifteen miles of Moscow. Stalin summoned Zhukov and asked him, "Are you sure we'll be able to hold Moscow? It hurts me to ask you that. Answer me truthfully, as a Communist."[20]

### Counterattack

Zhukov answered. Not only could the Soviets hold, but the Germans had extended themselves to such a degree that a counterattack would soon be possible. He was as good as his word. On December 6 the Soviets struck back with all the forces Zhukov could muster. A week later the Germans began withdrawing. Moscow radio reported that the assault on Moscow had failed. A furious Adolf Hitler announced he would assume personal command of all German forces.

The next summer the Germans struck to the south and by August were threatening the major city of Stalingrad. Should Stalingrad fall, the Germans could sweep east, cutting Soviet supply lines and capturing vital oil fields. On August 27 Stalin summoned Zhukov and outlined the danger. "How soon can you take off?"[21] he asked.

Zhukov went to Stalingrad with a new rank, deputy supreme commander in chief, the only such designation Stalin ever gave. When he arrived, the city was in danger of falling. By September 3 the Germans were within two miles. Later that month they entered the city itself and pushed the Soviets back toward the Volga River, which ran through the center of the city.

In mid-October the Germans launched an all-out offensive to take the city. Fierce fighting took place from street to street. Civilians were hurriedly formed into companies, given weapons, and rushed to the battle. By October 29 the German advance had been halted.

*Zhukov's soldiers storm an enemy position in the ruins of Stalingrad. In brutal street-to-street fighting, the Soviets blocked the Germans' advance into the city.*

The Germans, wrote Zhukov later, "were at the end of their strength."[22] He began gathering forces for a counterattack, which got under way on November 19 with a massive artillery barrage followed by an attack on the Germans' flanks. Now, instead of fighting to take Stalingrad, the Germans were fighting for their lives. Finally in February, after a month of bitter fighting and freezing cold, during which they had to slaughter Romanian cavalry horses for food, the Germans surrendered.

The Battle of Stalingrad was over. An estimated 800,000 soldiers of Germany and its allies had been killed. More than a million Soviet soldiers were dead, as well as hundreds of thousands of civilians. A German general, writing after the war, said, "In November I had told Hitler that if a quarter of a million soldiers were to be lost at Stalingrad, then the backbone of the entire Eastern Front would be broken. I was to be proved right, for the Battle of Stalingrad was the turning point of the entire war."[23]

## Soviet Marshal

Zhukov was made marshal of the Soviet Union, the first soldier ever to be so honored, but more work lay just ahead. His troops drove the Germans back some two hundred miles during the first months of 1943 and exhausted much of their strength. During the campaign a salient, or bulge, developed that stretched for 150 miles and protruded 100 miles into German-held territory around the city of Kursk.

The Germans, afraid that the Soviets would attack north from the salient toward Orel or south toward Kharkov, began to plan an attack designed to pinch off the bulge and trap the Soviet troops. Zhukov wanted to allow the Germans to attack and then counterattack. Later Zhukov wrote that Stalin "was afraid that our defenses might not be able to withstand the enemy onslaught. . . . This doubt continued, as I recall, until almost mid-May."[24]

Such was Zhukov's influence with Stalin that the Soviet dictator agreed. Zhukov anticipated where the Germans would attack and carefully prepared his defenses, principally antitank guns and minefields. On July 5, 1943, the Germans attacked. "At the very beginning of the offensive," German general F. W. von Mellenthin wrote later, "the piercing of the forward Russian lines . . . proved much more difficult than we anticipated. The terrific Russian counterattacks, with masses of men and material ruthlessly thrown in, were also an unpleasant surprise."[25]

Zhukov's strategy had worked. Hitler ordered the offensive halted, but it was too late. As Mellenthin described it: "We are now in the position of a man who has seized a wolf by the ears and dare not let him go."[26]

The Battle of Kursk—the largest tank battle in history with more than six thousand involved—was the end of the German offensive in the Soviet Union. Guns in Moscow fired victory salutes. Zhukov was showered with honors. Stalin wrote, "If the battle of Stalingrad foreshadowed the decline of the German fascist army, the battle of Kursk confronted it with disaster."[27]

## Halt at the Oder

The Soviets continued on the offensive, and by February 3, 1945, Zhukov's forces had crossed the Oder River, only fifty miles from Berlin. There, he halted. His harshest critic, fellow officer V. I. Chuikov, later claimed Zhukov could have taken Berlin by the end of the month. Zhukov disagreed, explaining, "I must say that the advance toward Berlin was not so simple as Chuikov thinks."[28]

At any rate, the advance resumed on Berlin. By now it was a race. The combined American and British forces were advancing from the west. Although Allied commander Dwight Eisenhower had promised Stalin that the Soviets would be allowed to take Berlin, Stalin didn't believe him.

Zhukov drove his troops without mercy, but west of Berlin he was stopped by fierce resistance from artillery fire from the Seelow Heights. Temporarily pinned down, he received a harsh telegram from Stalin. A reporter on hand at the time recalled that "Zhukov, a man with all the marks of an iron will about his face and a man who did not like to share his glory with anyone, was extremely worked up."[29]

He eventually was able to break through, however, and on April 30 his troops reached

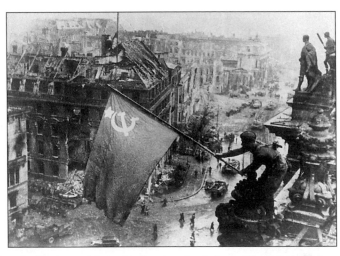

The Soviet flag is raised above the Reichstag in Berlin. Zhukov and his troops captured the German capitol on April 30, 1945.

the very center of Berlin, the Reichstag, or capitol building. At 3 P.M. Commander V. I. Kuznetsov radioed Zhukov: "Our Red Banner is on the Reichstag! Hurrah, Comrade Marshal!"[30]

The Soviet victory had been primarily due to the genius, stubbornness, and energy of Georgi Zhukov. Not only did he have a sound grasp of military situations, but he also had the will to force his opinion on others, even Joseph Stalin. Eisenhower, one of his greatest admirers, said in 1945, "One day there is certain to be another order of the Soviet Union. It will be the Order of Zhukov, and that order will be prized by every man who admires courage, vision, fortitude, and determination in a soldier."[31]

# Chapter 3

# Von Manstein: Hitler's Harshest Critic

**F**ield Marshal Erich von Manstein was a brilliant soldier whose hardest battles were not against his country's enemies, but against his country's leader, Adolf Hitler. After World War II he wrote, "On one side we had . . . a dictator who believed in the power of his will not only to nail down his armies wherever they might be but even to hold the enemy at bay. The same dictator, however, . . . lacked the groundwork of real military ability."[32]

Many a German general wrote the same thing about Hitler—after the war. Von Manstein not only said so to the Nazi leader's face, but did so repeatedly. As a result, Hitler relieved him of command in the Soviet Union in March 1944. Had von Manstein remained in charge, still disobeying Hitler when he felt it necessary, the end of World War II in Europe might have been postponed.

Hitler was never comfortable around von Manstein, an aristocratic Prussian whose ancestors had been military leaders for six hundred years and who, although personally loyal to Hitler as head of state, made no secret of his disdain for the Nazis. But von Manstein's often cold exterior hid a surprisingly modest personality. He was fond of saying that troops can usually do what they feel they can do and that his job was made easier by the morale of those he commanded. "Yes," said a general who served under him, "and when the Field-Marshal talked to the troops they always felt they could do what he asked."[33]

He was born Fritz Erich von Lewinski, tenth child of an artillery general, in 1887. Since his mother's sister, wife of infantry General Georg von Manstein, was childless, Erich's parents agreed that he would be adopted by the von Mansteins, whose name he took. With this family background, it was taken for granted that Erich would follow in the military tradition. Small wonder, then, that after five years in a preparatory school, von Manstein entered the corps of cadets at

## The Young Officer

In 1907, at the age of twenty, he was commissioned an officer in the Third Regiment of Foot Guards, one of the most prestigious units in the German army. Among its officers was Paul von Hindenburg, who would command German forces during World War I.

Von Manstein compiled an excellent record and in 1913 was selected to enter the *Kriegsakademie,* or war college, considered a training ground for future generals. His training was cut short, however, by the outbreak of World War I the next year.

During the war, von Manstein served as an adjutant, or assistant to the commanding officer, of a regiment in the Second Guards. He was seriously wounded during the first year of the war and spent the rest of the conflict as a staff officer, never getting a chance at command. In fact, he was fifty-three years old before he got an opportunity to command troops in battle during the invasion of France in 1940.

After World War I von Manstein remained in the German army, which had been shrunk by the peace treaty. With his knowledge, ability, and family connections, promotions came quickly. He refused to join an attempt in 1920 by some army officers to overthrow the new German republic,

*Erich von Manstein's greatest battles were fought against Adolf Hitler, not the enemy.*

the age of thirteen. His family connections, combined with his natural ability, made him stand out among his classmates, and he was chosen to be a page in the court of Kaiser Wilhelm II, the German emperor.

## Political Views

By 1936 he was a major general and deputy chief of staff to Field Marshal Werner von Fritsch. By this time, Hitler had been in power three years. Like most of the traditional German officers, von Manstein had mixed feelings about the Nazi leader. He appreciated what Hitler had done for the German economy and could not help but approve of his plans to build up the armed forces. He thought Hitler was crude, however, and detested both the Nazis and their racial ideas.

Despite his unquestioned loyalty, von Manstein was a difficult subordinate, constantly questioning and suggesting improvements to plans worked out by his superiors. Thus there was probably a feeling of relief in the high command when, after Hitler removed von Fritsch, von Manstein was transferred to an infantry division. Soon, however, he was again a staff officer, doing much of the planning for the invasion of Poland in 1939 by Field Marshal Gerd von Rundstedt.

When von Rundstedt went to France in November 1939 as commander of Army Group A, von Manstein went with him. Plans were being made for the invasion of France. Hitler and the high command drew up a plan based on Germany's strategy in World War I, an attack from the north through Holland and Belgium. Von Manstein thought the plan would be too obvious to the French and British and also had no clear-cut objective. He convinced von Rundstedt to present another plan, includ-

*In the years before World War I, von Manstein served as an officer in a prestigious regiment that also included future commander Paul von Hindenburg (pictured).*

writing later that the use of force against duly constituted government is counter to military tradition, regardless of what the military thinks of that government. He was to keep that same opinion years later when asked to join army plots against Adolf Hitler.

It was also in 1920 that he was married to Jutta Sybille, daughter of a wealthy landowner. They would have two sons, both of whom would be killed in action in World War II.

ing a surprise attack through the Ardennes Forest in order to cut off the enemy forces in Belgium.

It was a bold, brilliant plan. The Ardennes Forest was considered impenetrable by tanks and would be lightly defended. Yet, to the high command, it presented too much of a risk and was rejected. With von Rundstedt's permission, von Manstein sent a memorandum arguing for his plan to the high command. Von Rundstedt sent one directly to Hitler. Neither reached the Nazi leader.

## A New Assignment

Meanwhile, von Manstein was appointed commander of the Thirty-eighth Corps. He was told that he was now too senior to serve any longer in a staff position. Actually, he wrote, "it can hardly be doubted that my replacement was due to desire on the part of O.K.H. [the high command] to be rid of an importunate nuisance who had ventured to put up an operational plan at variance with its own."[34]

Fate soon intervened. A plane carrying a copy of the high command's plans was forced to land in Belgium, and the Germans had to assume their intentions were known. On February 17, 1940, von Manstein was in Berlin with other new corps commanders for a ceremony with Hitler. After the luncheon, Hitler invited von Manstein into his study and astounded him by asking him to outline his plan. Three days later the plan was approved. Once, during the war, when asked his

## Doing God's Work

Erich von Manstein was a devout Lutheran whose strong principles and sense of fairness made him turn away from the doctrine of racial hatred preached by Adolf Hitler and the Nazis. In 1934 he risked dismissal by refusing to carry out an order dismissing army officers who were part Jewish. In 1941 he refused to pass along Hitler's Commissar Order to execute every captured Communist Party official regardless of circumstances.

He regarded communism as a godless evil, and much of his efforts were to save his beloved Germany from a Soviet invasion. R. T. Paget, in his biography *Manstein*, quotes von Manstein as saying:

> For me the worst time was the Crimea. I knew for months on end that merely reasonable competence on the part of the Russians was all that was necessary to annihilate me and my army. I knew what happened to those who fell in Russian hands. I had seen the murdered wounded.

> This may seem odd to you, for you probably think that we were on devil's work and you may be right, but none the less it is true that at that time I had a mystic sense that I was in God's hands, and without this sense I could never have kept my nerve. Had I known of the abominations of the S.D. [*Sicherheisdienst*, or security service, responsible for rounding up and murdering thousands of Russian Jews] I could not have carried on, for I should have lost the support of God.

opinion of Hitler as a military leader, von Manstein joked, "Of course I formed a high opinion of Hitler's military good sense. He adopted my plan!"[35]

## The Commander in the Field

Von Manstein believed that a commander should spend as much time as possible on the front lines with his troops. In *Lost Victories*, he wrote:

> It gives him [the ordinary soldier] a certain satisfaction to see the Commanding General in the thick of it once in a while or watching a successful attack go in. Only by being with the fighting troops day in and day out can one get to know their needs, listen to their worries and be of assistance to them. A senior commander must not only be the man who perpetually has demands to make in the accomplishment of his mission; he must be an ally and a comrade as well.

Later in his memoirs, von Manstein gave this account of a typical day during the Panzer drive toward Leningrad in the summer of 1941. He later wrote that this was the most satisfying time of his military career:

> I myself slept in a sleeping-bag in the small tent I shared with my [aide] and do not remember having used a proper bed more than three times throughout this whole Panzer drive. . . . We always used to pitch our little camp in a wood or a copse near the main axis of advance—if possible by a lake or stream so that we could take a quick plunge before breakfast or whenever we came back caked with dust and grime from a trip to the front. . . . I usually left early in the morning, after receiving the dawn situation reports . . . to visit the forward troops. . . . By the time we returned to our tented camp, which would meanwhile have been shifted to a new location, we were dead tired and black as [chimney] sweeps.

With characteristic modesty, von Manstein discounts his role in the invasion of France. His role, he wrote, "was so insignificant that I could well afford to leave it out of these memoirs altogether." [36] The truth was somewhat different. Late in May 1940, this longtime staff officer got his first chance to command troops in battle and made the most of it. Ordered to hold a bridge on the Somme River, he instead went on the offensive, taking advantage of the weakness of the French forces opposite him.

The Thirty-eighth Corps overwhelmed the enemy, with von Manstein leading from the front lines rather than from the rear, dashing here and there in his staff car, encouraging his division commanders. "I have observed," he wrote, "that the field commander whose reaction is to wait for unimpeachable intelligence reports to clarify the situation has little hope of being smiled upon by the Goddess of War." [37]

### Crossing the Seine

Von Manstein roared on, pushing forward another forty miles in a single day. On June 6 the Thirty-eighth crossed the Seine River, the first German troops to do so. As the French fell back, he continued southward, reaching Le Mans on June 18 and crossing the Loire River on the 19th. The next day the French army surrendered.

That fall Hitler began to prepare to invade the Soviet Union. Von Manstein was named commander of the Fifty-sixth Panzer Corps being formed in Germany. He wrote, "For me this fulfilled a wish I had cherished even before the campaign in the west—to command a mechanized army corps."[38]

When the invasion was launched on June 22, von Manstein's unit attacked from East Prussia in the far northeast corner of Germany. Its objective was the city of Leningrad. As he had in France, von Manstein advanced rapidly.

Then, much to his frustration, he was ordered to stop so that the rest of the German units could catch up. "While this was certainly the 'safe,' staff-college solution," he wrote, "we had other ideas."[39] The worst thing for a tank corps on the march to do, he argued, was to stop. This gave the enemy time to build up forces.

By now, however, Hitler and the high command were in disagreement over strategy. Hitler wanted to take Leningrad in the north and the produce- and mineral-rich areas of the south. His generals wanted to move in the center and take Moscow. Hitler finally agreed, and the drive on Leningrad slowed down, with many of the units diverted for an attack on the Soviet capital.

Von Manstein, however, would not be part of that attack. He had been named to command the Eleventh Army far to the

*German troops advance into French territory during the invasion. Von Manstein modestly downplayed his role in the operation even though it was based on his plan.*

south, where his assignment was to clear the Crimean Peninsula of Soviet troops and to take the area to the north of the Sea of Azov. This was part of Hitler's grand strategy of capturing the key city of Stalingrad on the Volga River and moving on to seize the entire Caucasus Mountain region, thus shutting the Soviets off from the oil fields of the Persian Gulf. It was an important assignment, but one about which von Manstein had mixed feelings:

> Joyful though I was in taking over this new and bigger task, I was nevertheless fully aware that probably the most satisfying phase of my life as a soldier was now over. For three whole months I had lived close to the fighting troops, sharing not only their trials and tribulations, but also the pride of their successes. Time and again I had been able to derive fresh energy from the very fact of this common experience, from the cheerful devotion with which everyone went about his duty and from the intimacy of comradeship. From now on my position would prevent me from working among the troops to the extent I had done to date.[40]

## Victory in Crimea

After two months' hard fighting, all of Crimea had fallen except the city of Sebastopol on the western shore. Even though winter had begun and his troops were tired, von Manstein attacked the city. When Sebastopol finally fell on July 1, 1942, the Crimea was totally in German hands. Despite never having more than 350,000 soldiers, von Manstein had been able to take 450,000 Soviet prisoners. He was promoted to field marshal by Hitler.

It was during the Crimean campaign that an incident occurred that would result in von Manstein's later being tried as a war criminal. He signed an order that at one point called for elimination of the "Jewish-Bolshevist" system. After the war the Soviets claimed the order sanctioned the slaughter of Jews and others by special Nazi units.

In August von Manstein and the Eleventh Army were transferred back to the Leningrad area as part of an unsuccessful attempt to capture the city. He was there only three months before being ordered south again for what proved to be the most difficult and frustrating assignment of his career—Stalingrad.

The Germans had launched an all-out drive in October to capture Stalingrad and in fierce fighting had pushed their way through the western half of the city, pinning the Soviets against the Volga River. On November 19, however, the Red Army under Marshal Georgi Zhukov counterattacked from the northern and southern flanks of the German position. The Sixth Army of Field Marshal Friedrich Paulus was surrounded. Von Manstein's job was to rescue it.

Von Manstein tried to convince Hitler that the only hope for rescue was to have his forces attack the Soviets from the west while Paulus tried to break out of his trap from

*Soviet troops surrender to a German panzer crew. During the battle for the Crimea, von Manstein's Eleventh Army took 450,000 Soviet prisoners.*

the east. Hitler was furious. Not only was Stalingrad strategically important, but it bore the name of Hitler's worst enemy. "I won't leave the Volga!" he shouted at General Kurt Zeitzler, chief of the General Staff. "I won't go back from the Volga!"[41] Instead, he wanted von Manstein to attack through the Soviet encirclement, join Paulus, and occupy Stalingrad.

On November 28 von Manstein sent Hitler a full appraisal of the military situation. Paulus, he argued, must attempt to break out. Hitler did not reply for almost a week—"just one more example of the way Hitler loved to defer answers which were not to his taste,"[42] von Manstein wrote.

## Countermanding Hitler

Finally, on December 19, the exasperated von Manstein attempted to override Hitler. He sent an order directly to Paulus to attempt a breakout. By this time, however, Paulus had lost his nerve. He did not have enough fuel, he said, to make the attempt.

By late January Paulus's situation was desperate. He begged for permission to open surrender talks. Hitler refused. Instead, he said, the Sixth Army would "hold their positions to the last man and the last round."[43]

On February 2 Paulus surrendered. Distraught, von Manstein seriously considered resigning but decided to stay. "The soldier in the field is not in the pleasant position of the politician, who is always at liberty to climb off the band-wagon when things go wrong . . . ," he wrote. "The soldier has to fight where and when he is ordered."[44]

The Germans' entire southern front was now in danger. Von Manstein asked permission from Hitler to pull back. Hitler refused. On February 6 von Manstein flew to Hitler's headquarters and the two argued for six hours. He questioned the Nazi leader's military ability and suggested he relinquish everyday command to a chief of staff. "I was fully alive to the fact that Hitler would never be prepared to relinquish the supreme command officially," he wrote. "As a dictator he could not possibly have done so without suffering what for him would have been an intolerable loss of prestige."[45]

## Brilliance in Retreat

Throughout the spring of 1943, von Manstein fought a brilliant tactical campaign, often against Hitler's orders. He withdrew from the city of Kharkov, which Hitler had ordered held, only to recapture it in a maneuver one military historian called "one of the most masterly in the whole course of military history."[46] "Success proved me right, and Hitler had to tolerate my disobediences,"[47] von Manstein wrote.

By May a large Soviet salient, or bulge, around the city of Kursk had developed. Anticipating an attack from the salient, von Manstein proposed that the Germans take the initiative and attack first. Hitler agreed but delayed so long that Zhukov had built up strong defenses.

The Battle of Kursk was the largest tank battle in history and a crushing German defeat. Von Manstein had no choice but to begin to retreat. Hitler balked at every turn, refusing to allow ground to be given. Frustrated, von Manstein wrote to Zeitzler, "If the *Führer* [Hitler] thinks he can find any army group commander or headquarters staff . . . with the ability to foresee the inevitable more clearly than we have done, I am ready to hand over to them! As long as I remain at this post, however, I must have the chance to use my own head."[48]

Von Manstein would have to use his head frequently over the next few months. A British officer, Field Marshal Lord Carver, wrote, "The successful execution of the withdrawal [from the Don River to the Dnieper] under constant pressure, was a feat of military skill and resolution . . . which it is doubtful if any other Army could have equaled."[49]

And, as always, there were the battles with Hitler. Von Manstein wrote, "We lived, it seemed, in two entirely different worlds."[50] At a luncheon for senior officers on January 27, 1944, Hitler insulted them by saying, "If the end should come one day, it should really be the field marshals and generals who stand by the flags to the last." Unable to restrain himself, von Manstein called out, "And so they will, *mein Führer!*"[51]

*General Zhukov's armor races into action at Kursk, the largest tank battle in history. Although his forces suffered a crushing defeat, von Manstein was able to skillfully withdraw from the Soviet Union.*

Later the same day Hitler accused von Manstein of sending him letters on the military situation in order to "justify yourself to posterity in the war diary." Von Manstein replied that his personal letters to Hitler never went into his formal diary. "All I can say to your interpretation of my motives is that *I* am a gentleman."[52]

## The Final Argument

The final argument with Hitler came on March 25. Afterward von Manstein told one of Hitler's aides "that I considered it futile to remain in command . . . unless he accepted my recommendations."[53]

Von Manstein returned to the front. He had been there only a few days when Hitler sent for him. He was relieved of command, being told that "the time for grand-style operations in the east, for which I had been particularly qualified, was now past."[54] He never saw Hitler again.

For this soldier, the war was over. He retired to his estates. After the war British military historian Basil Liddell Hart wrote, "The ablest of the German generals was probably Field-Marshal Erich von Manstein. . . . He had a superb strategic sense, combined with a greater understanding of mechanized weapons than any of the generals who did not belong to the tank school itself."[55]

# Chapter 4

# Yamamoto: Reluctant Hero

**S**hortly after midnight on December 8, 1941, Yamamoto Isoroku, commander in chief of the Japanese fleet, sat alone in his cabin aboard his flagship about 160 miles south of Tokyo. Dipping his writing brush into a pot of his favorite Chinese ink, he wrote a brief poem:

> What does the world think?
> I do not care
> Nor for my life
> For I am the sword
> Of my Emperor.[56]

Halfway across the Pacific Ocean, across the international date line, it was early on the morning of December 7. Waves of airplanes, all bearing the rising sun insignia, headed for an attack on American installations at Pearl Harbor, Hawaii. Although the attack, which would plunge both Japan and the United States into World War II, was Yamamoto's brainchild, he had argued for years that to start a war with America would lead to the destruction of his country.

Yamamoto loved gambling above almost anything else and was as much at home playing bridge or poker as with traditional Japanese games of chance. This time, however, he was gambling with his country's future. He would win this gamble, but it would bring him no joy, and his prediction of the war's outcome would, unfortunately for Japan, come true.

He was born in 1884, the son of Sadakichi Tanako, a former samurai warrior who at the time was a poor village schoolmaster. Many years later, when he was thirty and both his parents were dead, he was, in keeping with Japanese custom, adopted by the prominent Yamamoto family. He thus changed his name to Yamamoto Isoroku (the family name coming first in Japan).

## Life in Nagaoka

Soon after his birth, his father obtained a better position as headmaster at a pri-

*Although he planned the attack on Pearl Harbor, Yamamoto Isoroku knew that Japan could not survive a prolonged war with America.*

mountain streams. When he was older, Yamamoto took a small boat onto the Sea of Japan, catching fish and octopus to help feed the family. It was at this time that he began to fall in love with the sea and come to know the wind and waves.

He also learned much from his father, who never tired of telling his young son about Japan's military history and the part his family had played. He also taught his son the art of calligraphy, and ink and brushes were one of the family's few luxuries.

Even though his family was better off than before, they were still poor. When Yamamoto began school, he could not afford textbooks and had to borrow them from classmates and copy them by hand.

Yamamoto was an excellent student and, although shorter than most boys his age, excelled at sports, especially baseball. He also developed an interest in and an appreciation of European-American culture. The Nagaoka area was one infrequently visited by foreigners, but an American missionary lived in a nearby town and Yamamoto and his brothers were permitted to visit him, learning history and a smattering of English.

His father's war stories and the missionary's descriptions of far-off lands made Yamamoto eager to see the world beyond Japan. When he was fifteen years old, he decided to try to gain admission into Japan's naval college. He took the entrance examination the next year, competing against three hundred other applicants. He did not think much of his chances and had decided

mary school in the city of Nagaoka near the western coast of Japan. Winters were so severe, with more than twelve feet of snow, that houses were virtually buried and people had to dig tunnels between dwellings. One of Yamamoto's first jobs was to help his older brothers shovel snow from the thatched roof of their house to prevent it from collapsing.

Much of the spring and summer, however, was spent out of doors—gathering mushrooms or fishing for salmon in the that if he was not accepted, he would become a schoolmaster like his father. He earned the second highest score on the exam, however, and entered the academy the same year.

## Rigorous Training

The training course for future naval officers lasted four years and was extremely rigorous. There were strict rules against smoking, alcohol, and dating. The punishment for breaking any rule was instant dismissal, but the cadets were so conditioned to obedience that such cases were rare.

Yamamoto graduated seventh in his class and had barely finished his training and been commissioned an ensign when war broke out between Japan and Russia. In the decisive Battle of Tsushima, he was wounded when, as he later wrote,

> with a great roar, a shell scored a direct hit on the forward eight-inch gun that still remained. Billows of acrid smoke covered the forward half of the vessel, and I felt myself almost swept away by a fierce blast. I staggered a few steps and found that the record charts that had been hanging round my neck had disappeared, and that two fingers of my left hand had been snapped off and were hanging by the skin alone.[57]

Japan was not a party to World War I, so the years when much of Europe was in tumult passed quietly for the young naval officer. In 1910 he married the daughter of a dairy farmer and started a family. There was respect but little passion between Yamamoto and his wife, Reiko. The great love of his life was Kikuji, a geisha, or hostess, whom he would meet in 1934.

There were promotions along the way and a variety of assignments, including his first voyage to the United States as part of a diplomatic mission in 1910 only a few months after his marriage. He took a very early interest in aviation and in 1915 told a reporter, "The most important warship of the future will be a ship to carry airplanes."[58]

## Yamamoto's Personality

Yamamoto was studious and attentive to his duties but had an unpredictable and

*Japanese warships (foreground) shell the Russian fleet during the Battle of Tsushima. Yamamoto lost two fingers during the engagement.*

almost childlike sense of fun completely at odds with his usual demeanor. Once, when a passenger on an ocean liner as a young man, he thought a party needed enlivening, so he did a handstand on a stair rail in full evening dress. Years later, as an admiral, he was seated next to an army officer who was standing and giving a long-winded speech. Inch by inch, Yamamoto slid the army officer's chair backward so that when the officer finally went to sit, he sprawled unceremoniously on the floor.

Yamamoto's great passion was gambling. He once told an admiral, "If only you'd give me a couple of years amusing myself in Europe, I'd earn you the money for at least a couple of battleships."[59]

In 1919 Yamamoto was sent to the United States for a two-year course at Harvard University to study oil exploration and production. He became such an expert on oil production that several American companies offered him jobs. While at Harvard he also served as an aide to the Japanese ambassador at the Washington, D.C., disarmament conference at which Japan was limited to a fleet 60 percent the size of those of the United States and Great Britain.

On his return to Japan, he became director of a new pilot training school, learning to fly along with recruits half his age. He drove his students hard. There were many accidents and many fatalities, but Yamamoto was determined that Japanese pilots would be second to none. Recruits would be brought into his office and shown

## A Razor-Sharp Spear

Matsunaga Keisuke, an aide to Yamamoto at the time he was naval vice minister, gave this description of the admiral's command style. It is found in *The Reluctant Admiral* by Hiroyuki Agawa:

Where [navy minister Mitsumasa] Yonai was an ax, Yamamoto was a spear. I feel that he had a unique sensitivity toward the workings of each of his subordinate's minds. He would never bawl any of them out, but there was always an intimidating sense that he could read what one was thinking. You only had to be with him for a little while to recognize that he was no ordinary person. People often ask me if it wasn't difficult to work under somebody as razor-sharp as he, but I never felt so in the slightest. At parties and so on, although he didn't touch alcohol, he would unbend even more than others who were drunk. His one fault, perhaps, is that he seems to have been what you might call very unsentimental, not to say harsh, where army people or personal rivals were concerned.

plaques honoring those who had been killed. "The Naval Air Corps will probably never be really strong until the whole wall . . . is plastered with names like these,"[60] he told them.

In 1925 he returned to the United States, this time as naval attaché at the Japanese embassy in Washington. He continued to study naval aviation. U.S. Navy captain Ellis Zacharias, who knew Yamamoto at the time, later said, "The aircraft carrier, the combination of sea power and air power, was an obsession with Yamamoto.

. . . I always felt that the first plans for the Pearl Harbor attack originated in his restless brain right here in Washington."[61]

## The London Conference

Yamamoto returned to Japan in 1928, and after assignments as captain of a cruiser and the aircraft carrier *Akagi*, he went to London as part of the Japanese delegation to another disarmament conference, this time as a rear admiral. He was successful in gaining for Japan equality with the United States and Britain in light cruisers and submarines, but the 60 percent rule for heavier vessels remained.

After the London talks, Yamamoto was named head of the technical division of the navy's aeronautics department. Here, he was able to influence the development of the airplanes that would give Japan control of the skies over the Pacific in the early months of World War II, including the famous Zero fighter and the Type 96 land-based bomber. He was convinced that airpower would be the key element of the next war. While most of his colleagues still claimed that only a battleship could sink another battleship, Yamamoto said, "Torpedo planes can do it. The fiercest serpent may be overcome by a swarm of ants."[62]

In 1934 he went to talks in London once more, this time as a vice admiral in charge of the Japanese delegation. As soon as he arrived, Yamamoto said, "Japan can no longer submit to the ratio system. There is no possibility of compromise by my government on that point."[63] When he returned to Japan, he was a national hero for having stood up to the British and Americans.

Some officers began to talk openly of a war with the United States. Yamamoto had doubts. He was opposed to such a war and said so, and when he did, right-wing groups threatened him with assassination. "I am serving my country just as if I were commanding in action," he said. "I am fighting a battle to bring my countrymen round to a sensible way of thinking. They can kill me—but they can't kill that."[64]

## Personal Doubts

Yamamoto knew from personal experience that the United States had a far superior industrial base and that Japan was bound to lose a prolonged war. "If we are ordered to do it," he said to the Japanese prime minister in 1940, "then I guarantee to put up a tough fight for the first six months, but I have absolutely no confidence as to what would happen if it went on for two or three years."[65]

By this time, however, war seemed inevitable, and Yamamoto, now commander in chief of the entire Japanese fleet, began to think how best to fight the war he had hoped would not come. He thought that Japan's best chances lay in a massive strike at the main U.S. fleet at Pearl Harbor. Furthermore, he thought a surprise attack had an even better chance of success.

Superiors in the navy department and the Japanese government were against the plan. Hawaii was too far from Japan, they said. There was no way to achieve surprise.

Finally, in October 1941 Yamamoto sent Rear Admiral Kamahito Kuroshima to Tokyo to talk to the naval general staff. When they still opposed the attack, Kuroshima left the room to telephone Yamamoto. When he returned he said, "I have the authority of the Commander-in-Chief to tell you if you do not agree to his plan he must resign from his position and retire into civilian life."[66] The admirals gave in.

On November 25 the task force sailed east, commanded by Vice Admiral Chuichi

*Pearl Harbor is seen here two months before the air raid. Yamamoto believed that Japan's only hope for victory over the United States lay in a surprise knockout blow against its Pacific fleet.*

Nagumo, senior carrier commander. Yamamoto remained behind on the *Nagato*. He wrote to a friend, "What a strange position I find myself in now—having to make a decision diametrically opposed to my personal opinion, with no choice but to push full speed in pursuance of that decision."[67]

## A Sour Victory

The attack on Pearl Harbor was a huge success, one that set off a frenzied celebration in Japan and made Yamamoto even more of a hero. He found it impossible to celebrate. For one thing, having struck at an unsuspecting enemy bothered his sense of honor. For another, he

knew, despite this success, what might lie ahead. He wrote his sister, "Well, war has begun at last. But in spite of all the clamour that is going on we could lose it. I can only do my best."[68]

Pearl Harbor was only the first of a series of Japanese victories. Three days after Pearl Harbor, Yamamoto's land-based bombers

### "A Sleeping Enemy"

Yamamoto was deeply disturbed over the fact that his aircraft had attacked Pearl Harbor when no declaration of war had taken place. As a result, he could not freely join in the national celebration that followed the victory. In fact, he was embarrassed at the accolades he received, as revealed in this letter quoted in *The Reluctant Admiral* by Hiroyuki Agawa:

Thank you for your kind letter of New Year's Day [1942]. A military man can scarcely pride himself on having "smitten a sleeping enemy"; in fact, to have it pointed out is more a matter of shame. I would rather you made your appraisal after seeing what the enemy does,

since it is certain that, angered and outraged, he will soon launch a determined counterattack, whether it be a full-scale engagement on the sea, air raids on Japan itself, or a strong attack against the main units of our fleet. Either way, my one desire is to carry through the first stage of operations before the enemy can recover, and, on the surface at least, achieve some basis for a protracted war.

---

*The USS* Shaw *explodes after being hit by a bomb. Yamamoto regretted that the attack on Pearl Harbor took place before war was declared.*

sank the British battleships *Repulse* and *Prince of Wales*. Yamamoto showed much more excitement and pleasure with this feat than with Pearl Harbor. This had not been a sneak attack, but one against battleships on full alert. His long advocacy of airpower had been proved correct.

More triumphs followed. Drunk with victory, the Japanese government wanted to expand the war. Yamamoto instead urged a negotiated peace that would allow Japan to hold what it had conquered. He was ignored. "It is not so hard to open a war as to conclude it,"[69] he ruefully told a friend.

With the government insisting on another major offensive, Yamamoto proposed to capture Midway Island, the closest American base to Japan. He reasoned that the United States would send everything left in its fleet to defend it, giving Japan a chance to win a decisive sea battle.

Just as with Pearl Harbor, most of the naval staff admirals opposed the plan, but Yamamoto held firm. On May 27 an attack force of nineteen ships, including four carriers, sailed from Hiroshima. Once more, Admiral Nagumo was in command. The operation was a disaster in which almost everything possible went wrong for the Japanese, and their four carriers were sunk. The defeat shook Yamamoto. When one of his younger officers asked how the navy would apologize to the emperor, Yamamoto snapped, "Leave that to me. I am the only one who must apologize to His Majesty."[70] He then went to his cabin and was not seen for several days.

The Battle of Midway made Yamamoto's worst fears a reality. Japan no longer had an advantage in terms of ships, and he knew the United States, with its vastly greater industrial capacity, would rapidly overtake his fleet. He no longer had the resources for a major offensive in the central Pacific, so he decided to move south, cooperating with the army in a plan to move within striking distance of Australia.

## Attack on Guadalcanal

In July 1942, from their base in Rabaul in New Britain, the Japanese landed troops on Guadalcanal in the Solomon Islands, about eight hundred miles closer to Australia, and began building an airfield. By February 1943, however, Yamamoto could not adequately supply the Guadalcanal troops, and they were evacuated, many sick and starving. The defeat was a tremendous blow to Japanese morale. Yamamoto felt the need to make a personal trip to the frontline bases to give his troops encouragement, even though he knew in his heart that the war was lost. A few weeks earlier, at the start of the new year, he had written a poem:

Looking back over the year
I feel myself grow tense
At the number of comrades
Who are no more.[71]

On April 13 the itinerary for Yamamoto's tour was sent out as a radio message. The selected bases knew exactly when and where he would visit. So did the Americans.

Years before the start of the war, the United States had broken the Japanese code. Now, news of Yamamoto's trip was taken to his American counterpart, Admiral Chester Nimitz, at Pearl Harbor. Nimitz studied the message and said, "What do you say? Do we try to get him?"[72] He was afraid that an ambush attempt would reveal to the Japanese that their code had been broken, but he decided to take the chance.

## On Dying for One's Country

No matter what he thought of his country's war with the United States, Admiral Yamamoto remained steadfastly loyal to his country and its emperor. His strong sense of duty is reflected in this document, written in May 1939, when he was threatened with assassination for his opposition to the coming war. It was found in a safe in his office after his death in 1943 and is quoted in *The Reluctant Admiral* by Hiroyuki Agawa:

> To give up his life for his sovereign and country is the military man's most cherished wish: what difference whether he give it up at the front or behind the lines? To die valiantly and gloriously in the heat of battle is easy; yet who knows how hard it is to die for one's convictions, in the teeth of popular censure? Ah, how lofty is the sovereign's benevolence, how enduring his nation! All that matters is the Empire's far-ranging policies; personal glory or shame, death or survival, are of no import. As Confucius says: "One may crush cinnabar, yet not take away its color; one may burn the fragrant herb, yet not take away its scent." They may destroy my body, yet not take away my will.

## Ambushed

At 6 A.M. on April 18, two Type 1 bombers took off from Rabaul carrying Yamamoto and members of his staff. At almost the same time, a squadron of American P-38 fighters, specially equipped with extra fuel tanks, took off from Guadalcanal.

At 9:34 A.M., flying just above the waves, the American pilots spotted Yamamoto's planes approaching the island of Bougainville. When the Japanese pilots saw the Americans, they immediately dived toward the island, hoping their aircrafts' camouflage would hide them when they were over the jungle. P-38 pilot Lieutenant Thomas Lanphier locked on to the lead bomber, opening fire with his 37-millimeter cannon and .50-caliber machine guns. Smoke began coming from the bomber, then flames. Admiral Matomi Ugaki, in the second bomber, which was also shot down but managed a crash landing—later remembered what he saw:

> For a few minutes I lost sight of Yamamoto's plane but finally located it far to the right. I was horrified to see it flying slowly just above the jungle with bright orange flames rapidly enveloping the wings and the fuselage. About four miles from us the bomber trailed thick, black smoke, dropping lower and lower. As our bomber snapped out of its turn I scanned the jungle. The plane was no longer in sight. Black smoke boiled from the dense jungle into the air.[73]

The next day a search party led by a Lieutenant Hamasuna, who had not been told whom he was seeking, found the remains of the plane. Still strapped into its seat, one hand gripping a sword, was a body. The hand gripping the sword had three fingers. Hamasuna knew he had found Yamamoto.

Yamamoto Isoroku, Japan's most outstanding military leader, was dead. He would not see the final defeat of Japan that he had predicted, but to the last he had

*A formation of P-38 fighters patrols the waters surrounding Guadalcanal. Yamamoto was killed when his plane was ambushed and shot down by a similar flight.*

been faithful to his soldier's oath. Just a few days prior to his fatal flight, he had written:

I am still the sword
Of my Emperor.
It will not be sheathed
Until I die.[74]

# Chapter 5

# MacArthur: "I Shall Return"

There is no denying that Douglas MacArthur was vain, arrogant, and notoriously self-serving. He was also, however, a brilliant tactician who accomplished more with fewer resources and with less loss of life than any major commander in World War II. Great Britain's senior general, Field Marshal Viscount Alan Brooke, wrote that MacArthur "outshone Marshall, Eisenhower and all the other American and British generals including Montgomery."[75]

MacArthur began the war commanding the single greatest defeat in the history of the United States military—the loss of the Philippine Islands and the Japanese capture of seventy thousand American and Filipino soldiers, many of whom would die en route to or inside prison camps. He ended it by accepting the unconditional surrender of Japan aboard the battleship *Missouri* in Tokyo Harbor. In between he fought not only the Japanese, but his superiors in Washington, the U.S. Navy, his Australian allies, and even the president of the United States.

MacArthur's military record would have to have been spectacular, indeed, to equal that of his father. Arthur MacArthur enlisted in the Twenty-fourth Wisconsin Infantry at the age of seventeen during the American Civil War. By the age of twenty he was colonel of the regiment, and his valor at the Battle of Missionary Ridge won him a Congressional Medal of Honor.

In 1875 he married Mary Pinckney Hardy. Douglas, their third son, was born on an army post in Little Rock, Arkansas, on January 26, 1880. Shortly afterward his father was named commander of Fort Wingate in the northwest New Mexico Territory. Douglas's first six years were spent there and at Fort Selden near the Mexican border. The remote outposts were hard on his mother, but Douglas loved the frontier life. He later wrote, "I learned to ride and shoot even before I could read or write."[76]

There were no schools, so his mother and father tutored him, using the few books available. He also closely observed how his father and the troop's first sergeant, Peter Ripley, handled the soldiers under them. He absorbed some of the techniques of command that he would later put to good use.

## Back to Civilization

In 1886 MacArthur's father was transferred to Fort Leavenworth, Kansas. Dou-

*Only his tactical brilliance and victories in the battles of the South Pacific matched Douglas MacArthur's arrogance and vanity.*

glas had to leave the carefree frontier life behind and enter public school, wearing high-top shoes, shirt, and tie instead of roaming barefoot through the New Mexico sagebrush. He was at best an average student in Kansas and in Washington, D.C., his father's next assignment.

MacArthur's education did an about-face in 1893 when his father was posted at Fort Sam Houston in San Antonio, Texas. Douglas was enrolled at the nearby West Texas Military Academy and promptly began to excel, adapting quickly to the strict regimen. When he graduated in 1897, he was near the top of his class and was the most outstanding athlete in the school.

He spent the next year and a half preparing for the entrance examination to West Point, on which he far outdistanced other applicants. He entered the academy in June 1899. His father had been ordered to the Philippine Islands, and his mother went with Douglas to West Point, living at a hotel near the campus.

MacArthur excelled just as much at West Point as he had at military school. He was a good athlete, popular with his classmates, and much admired by girls who attended the dances, or "hops," at West Point and considered him the most handsome cadet in the corps.

He did even better in the classroom, graduating from West Point

*While at West Point, MacArthur earned the third highest academic average in the academy's history.*

in 1903 with an academic average of 98.14, the third highest average in the history of the academy and the highest since the 98.33 earned by Robert E. Lee seventy-four years earlier. On his commissioning as a second lieutenant, he was assigned to an engineering battalion in the Philippines, from which his father had just returned. In 1904, when his father was once again ordered to the Far East, Douglas joined him as an aide. For nine months he toured India, Java, and Japan, becoming thoroughly familiar with Asian thinking and military tactics in the course of his travels.

## Various Assignments

The next ten years saw MacArthur in a variety of assignments, everything from President Theodore Roosevelt's military aide to press censor to advising on fortifications around the recently built Panama Canal. On an expeditionary force to Veracruz, Mexico, he came under fire from a band of rebels and acted so courageously that he was recommended for a Medal of Honor. The recommendation was denied by the War Department, so MacArthur still had yet to equal his father in that respect.

When the United States entered World War I in 1917, MacArthur was promoted to colonel and made chief of staff of the Rainbow Division, so-called because it contained elements of national guard units from every state. He had only been in France a few weeks when he led a small party in the capture of a German machine gun position. He was awarded the French Croix de Guerre and the American Silver Star, the first of more than two dozen decorations he would earn during the war.

MacArthur's fame aroused the jealousy of some of his brother officers. They complained to General John J. "Black Jack" Pershing about his going unarmed, refusing to wear a helmet or gas mask, and his insistence at being at the front of his troops instead of commanding from the rear, as was customary. Finally, Pershing had enough. "Stop all this nonsense," he said. "MacArthur is the greatest leader of troops we have, and I intend to make him a division commander."[77]

In addition to observing MacArthur's action in the field, Pershing had been receiving letters from Mary MacArthur urging that her son be promoted to general. On July 11, 1918, Pershing agreed, and MacArthur got his first star. Shortly afterward he left the Rainbow Division's headquarters staff to command one of its brigades, the Eighty-fourth.

He eventually was named commander of the Rainbow Division, but the war ended before a recommended promotion to major general was confirmed. He was also disappointed that although he was one of the most decorated American soldiers of World War I, he still did not receive the Medal of Honor for which Pershing recommended him after the storming of Châtillon by the Eighty-fourth Brigade.

## After the War

After the war, although many officers were reduced in rank as part of the shrinking army, MacArthur retained his general's star

*During World War I, MacArthur stands in France with members of the Rainbow Division. He earned more than two dozen decorations during the war.*

and landed an important appointment as superintendent of West Point, instituting some badly needed reforms. In 1922 he returned to the Philippines as a division commander. One of his projects was to draw up a plan for defending the Bataan Peninsula enclosing Manila Bay, an exercise that would be put to good use in World War II.

Some people whispered that MacArthur's assignment to the Philippines was a result of his marriage to Louise Cromwell Brooks. Among the other suitors of the wealthy divorcée had been General Pershing, now army chief of staff, and some saw the assignment as a banishment, a charge on which MacArthur remained silent and that was hotly denied by Pershing.

MacArthur's mother disapproved of the marriage and, partly because of the tensions her disapproval created, the couple were divorced in 1929. MacArthur's second marriage, to Jean Marie Faircloth a few months after his mother's death in 1936, was much happier and would last until MacArthur's death.

After becoming the youngest two-star general in the history of the army in 1924, he served as a corps commander in the United States from 1925 to 1927 and in 1928 took a temporary assignment as president of the U.S. Olympic Committee, overseeing the preparation of the American team. He returned to the Philippines later that year as commander of all U.S. forces. Like others, he was taking note of increased militarism in Japan and began thinking about the possibility of a Japanese invasion of the islands.

## Chief of Staff

In 1930 MacArthur was appointed by President Herbert Hoover to be chief of staff, the highest rank in the army and one that made him a four-star general. He was now fifty years old and the youngest man ever to serve in that post. The 1930s, however, were not the best years to head the army. Military budgets were repeatedly cut, and most Americans wanted nothing more to do with war. MacArthur had little patience with pacifism. "Pacifist habits do not insure peace or immunity," he wrote. "For the sentimentalism and emotionalism which have

*MacArthur married his second wife, Jean Marie Faircloth, in 1936. Their union would last for almost twenty-eight years.*

infested our country we should substitute hard common sense. We should at all times be prepared to defend ourselves."[78]

When his term as chief of staff ended in 1935, he was appointed by President Franklin Roosevelt as special military adviser to the Philippines, which were due to be granted full independence in 1946. On his staff was a young lieutenant colonel named Dwight Eisenhower.

In July 1941 the threat from Japan was growing. Roosevelt recalled MacArthur to active duty, appointing him commander of all army forces in the Far East, including the Filipino forces he had developed. Nevertheless, MacArthur was not prepared when the attack came. Although he knew of the assault on Pearl Harbor nine hours before the Japanese attacked the Philippines, he inexplicably took no steps to protect his aircraft, most of which were destroyed as they sat on the ground.

With most of their air strength gone, the Philippines were vulnerable to invasion, which began on December 10, two days after the air strike. It quickly became evident that the islands would be overrun. In January 1942 MacArthur skillfully withdrew all American forces and most of the Filipino troops on the island of Luzon onto the Bataan Peninsula, where he hoped to hold on until help arrived from the United States.

That help never arrived. Eisenhower, now a general in Washington, told Chief of Staff George Marshall, "General, it will be a long time before major reinforcements can

## Doug's Communiqués

MacArthur's ego was such that he minimized any setback and exaggerated any victory. This was evident in the series of communiqués sent from Australia during the war in New Guinea. These communiqués reflected not only MacArthur's vanity, but the willingness of his staff to draft messages that wildly inflated American successes while dismissing the ability of the Japanese and even the contributions of the Australians. While the American public believed these stories, they caused widespread resentment among the troops, one of whom penned this unflattering poem, found in *MacArthur as Military Commander* by Gavin Long:

> Here, too, is told the saga bold,
>     of virile, deathless youth
> In stories seldom tarnished with
>     the plain, unvarnished truth.
> It's quite a rag, it waves the flag,
>     Its motif is the fray,
> And modesty is plain to see in
>     Doug's Communiqué . . .
>
> "My battleships bombard the Nips from
>     Maine to Singapore;
> My subs have sunk a million tons;
>     They'll sink a billion more.
> My aircraft bombed Berlin last night,"
>     In Italy they say
> "Our turn's tonight, because it's right in
>     Doug's Communiqué . . ."
>
> And while possibly a rumor now,
>     someday it will be fact
> That the Lord will hear a deep voice say
>     "Move over, God—it's Mac."
> So bet your shoes that all the news
>     that last great Judgment Day
> Will go to press in nothing less than
>     DOUG'S COMMUNIQUÉ!

get to the Philippines. . . . Our base must be Australia."[79] Roosevelt, however, continued to send MacArthur messages saying that help was on the way. When it became clear that the Philippines were to be abandoned, MacArthur was furious, believing that Roosevelt, the navy, and the War Department in Washington were all out to get him. Three years later, when the president died, MacArthur said to an aide, "So Roosevelt is dead: a man who would never tell the truth when a lie would serve him just as well."[80]

MacArthur's staff is seen here in a tunnel on Corregidor. His troops gave MacArthur the nickname "Dugout Doug" because he rarely left the island fortress.

## "Dugout Doug"

MacArthur's troops, however, blamed their commander, who spent almost all his time on the fortress island of Corregidor rather than with them on Bataan. They called him "Dugout Doug" and wrote a song to the tune of the "Battle Hymn of the Republic," one verse of which went:

Dugout Doug, come out from hiding
Dugout Doug, come out from hiding
Send to Franklin the glad tidings
That his troops go starving on![81]

Roosevelt might abandon the Philippines, but he couldn't abandon MacArthur. The beleaguered general was a hero to the American public, and his death or capture would be a severe blow to morale. In March the president ordered MacArthur to be evacuated from the Philippines and go to Australia, where he would take command of all Allied forces. MacArthur, who had planned to die with his troops, somewhat reluctantly agreed.

On March 20 in Adelaide, Australia, he made his first public statement:

> The President of the United States ordered me to break through the Japanese lines and proceed from Corregidor to Australia for the purpose, as I understand it, of organizing the American offensive against Japan, a primary objective of which is the relief of the Philippines. I came through and I shall return.[82]

The War Department had tried to convince him to change the final phrase to "we shall return," but MacArthur refused. It was both an example of his immense ego and also his spite at what he considered a betrayal by Washington of his men in the Philippines.

It would be a long time, however, before he could return. There were some pleasant surprises awaiting him in Australia. He had been promoted to the newly created rank of five-star general, and he had been awarded the Congressional Medal of Honor, finally equaling his father. The forces under his command, however, were pitifully few and meagerly equipped. Furthermore, the Australians were proposing to abandon most of the northern and western parts of the continent to the Japanese and defend a line running from Brisbane to Perth.

## On the Offensive

MacArthur was aghast. He knew from his Philippines experience that it would be a disastrous mistake to sit back and wait for a Japanese invasion. "Never let the [Japanese] attack you," he said. "When the Japanese soldier has a coordinated plan of attack he works smoothly. When *he* is attacked—when he doesn't know what is coming—it isn't the same."[83] Instead of waiting, he told his surprised staff, he would carry the fight to the Japanese, moving north to the island of New Guinea.

*American troops come ashore at New Guinea. MacArthur knew that only offensive tactics, not defensive ones, would be effective against the Japanese.*

After halting a Japanese advance on the city of Port Moresby, MacArthur went on the offensive with a goal of taking the city of Buna on the northern coast. His green American troops, however, were unequal to the task. He removed the American field commander and replaced him with General Robert Eichelberger. "Go out there, Bob, and take Buna," he told Eichelberger, "or don't come back alive."[84] Buna fell to Allied troops on January 11, 1943, and MacArthur had his precious foothold on the northern coast of New Guinea.

By now there were two supreme commanders in the Pacific. MacArthur maintained a deep resentment of the navy. The navy, likewise, seemed to be against any plan he proposed. Secretary of War Henry Stimson wrote in his diary that "the extraordinary brilliance of that officer [MacArthur] is not always matched by his tact, but the Navy's astonishing bitterness against him seems childish."[85] The solution reached by Roosevelt was that MacArthur would be supreme commander in the South Pacific and Admiral Chester Nimitz in the Central Pacific.

MacArthur's plan was to move northwest along New Guinea, simply going around major Japanese strongholds, leaving them to wither from lack of supplies rather than meeting them head-on. It was the strategy the Japanese feared most, as General Matsuichi Ino later wrote:

The Americans attacked and seized, with minimum losses, a relatively weak area, constructed air fields and then proceeded to cut the supply lines to our troops in that area. Our strongpoints were gradually starved out. The Japanese Army preferred direct assault after the German fashion, but the Americans flowed into our weaker points and submerged us, just as water seeks the weakest entry to sink a ship.[86]

## Competing Strategies

By June 1944 MacArthur's forces were only about 300 miles south of the Philippine island of Mindanao. At the same time, Nimitz's marines were 1,400 miles from the Philippines but only about the same distance from Japan. Nimitz argued that the Philippines should be bypassed and a major campaign mounted against the island of Formosa, only 700 miles from Japan. At a meeting in Hawaii with Nimitz and President Roosevelt, MacArthur argued passionately that to abandon the Filipinos a second time "could not be condoned or forgiven."[87] Overwhelmed by the arguments and the force with which they were made, Roosevelt decided in MacArthur's favor. Before going to bed, the president asked his physician for an aspirin. "In fact," he added, "give me another aspirin to take in the morning. In all my life nobody has ever talked to me the way MacArthur did."[88]

On October 20, 1944, MacArthur made good on his promise of March 1942. Four hours after the first troops were landed on the island of Leyte, he stepped from a barge into knee-deep water and strode onto

*MacArthur and Admiral Chester Nimitz (with pointer) meet with President Roosevelt in Hawaii to discuss strategy. MacArthur was able to convince the president not to bypass the Philippines.*

Philippine soil. While his nervous troops watched for snipers, MacArthur used a communications truck to broadcast a radio message, "People of the Philippines: I have returned. . . . Rally to me!"[89]

The fight for the Philippines was long and deadly. Mindoro was invaded in December and the principal island, Luzon, in January. Manila fell to the Americans on February 3. The final victory would take another six months. MacArthur was constantly at the scene of the heaviest fighting, ignoring both the bullets that whined around him and the pleas of his staff for him to take cover.

As operations in the Philippines were winding down; plans were under way for the invasion of the main Japanese islands. Nimitz would command the landing, tentatively scheduled for November. MacArthur would command the soldiers once ashore. All these plans, however, were unnecessary.

## War's End

In late July General Thomas Farrell came to Manila from Washington to see MacArthur, who lectured his visitor about the upcoming invasion for almost fifteen

## Bittersweet Return

After MacArthur returned to the Philippines, as his troops were fighting to recapture Manila from the Japanese, the general went to a prison at Bilibid that had recently been liberated. Many of the freed prisoners had been with MacArthur on Bataan three years earlier. As he made his way among them, many of the men, barely skeletons after years in captivity, tried to come to attention for their former commander. MacArthur's recollection of the incident is found in *American Caesar* by William Manchester:

> They remained silent, as though at inspection. I looked down the lines of men bearded and soiled . . . with ripped and soiled shirts and trousers, with toes sticking out of such shoes as remained, with suffering and torture written on their gaunt faces. Here was all that was left of my men of Bataan and Corregidor. . . . As I passed down the scrawny, suffering column, a murmur accompanied me as each man barely speaking above a whisper, said, "You're back," or "You made it" . . . I could only reply, "I'm a little late, but we finally came." I passed on out of the barracks compound and looked around at the debris that was no longer important to those inside: the tin cans they had eaten from; the dirty old bottles they had drunk from. It made me ill just to look at them.

minutes before finally asking Farrell why he had come. As Farrell said later, "I swallowed and told him we had developed the atomic bomb and would he please keep all of his planes out of the general area of Hiroshima around the end of the first week of August."[90]

The atomic bomb brought the war to a halt, and MacArthur signed the surrender document on behalf of the Allies on September 2, 1945. Afterward, MacArthur spoke to a worldwide radio audience:

> A great victory has been won. . . . The entire world is entirely at peace. The holy mission has been completed. And in reporting this to you, the people, I speak for the thousands of silent lips, forever stilled among the jungles and the beaches and in the deep waters of the Pacific which marked the way.[91]

Of all the commanders of World War II, Douglas MacArthur was, without a doubt, the most conceited and egotistical. "You don't have a staff, General," George Marshall once told him. "You have a court."[92] These same qualities, however, also gave him a sense of destiny and a limitless self-confidence. Perhaps nothing less could have led him through the dark days of Bataan, back to the Philippines, and finally to Tokyo Harbor.

# Chapter 6

# Nimitz: The Quiet Hero

**T**here was little to mark Chester W. Nimitz as a warrior. With his calm, cheerful demeanor and a friendly face topped by a thatch of snow-white hair, he seemed more like a kindly grandfather than the commander of a vast armada. Those who served under him knew, however, that there was steel beneath the softness. This firmness, tempered with patience and humor, enabled him to mold and direct the Allied victory over Japan in World War II.

Nimitz was neither flamboyant nor impetuous, like some of his contemporaries. He had no nickname such as "Bull" (Halsey), "Terrible" (Thompson), or "Howling Mad" (Smith). In December 1941, with most of its fleet sunk or damaged at Pearl Harbor, the last thing the U.S. Navy needed was a hothead who might lose what remained and leave the West Coast open to attack. Instead, the navy needed Nimitz, a quiet voice of authority to rebuild the shattered fleet, rejuvenate the shattered morale

of its sailors, and slowly but surely turn the tide of battle.

Fredericksburg, a tiny, remote German-American farming community deep in the hill country of Texas, seems an unlikely birthplace for an admiral. Nimitz, in fact, never saw the ocean until he enrolled in the U.S. Naval Academy at Annapolis, Maryland. His family background, however, had both military and maritime elements. Among his ancestors were members of the Germanic Knights of the Sword and Knights of the Teutonic Order in the Middle Ages.

Nimitz's grandfather and great-grandfather, both named Karl Heinrich Nimitz, served in the German merchant marine and eventually emigrated to Charleston, South Carolina. Karl Heinrich Jr. moved on to help found Fredericksburg and changed his name to Charles Henry Nimitz.

Nimitz's grandfather never lost his love for the sea. The front of the hotel he built on Fredericksburg's Main Street was shaped like the bow of a ship. After his grandson, the future admiral, was born in 1885, he would regale the youngster with sea stories. Nimitz later wrote:

> I didn't know my father, because he died before I was born, but I had a wonderful white-bearded grandfather. . . . Between chores and homework I listened wide-eyed to stories about his youth in the German merchant marine. "The sea—like life itself—is a stern taskmaster," he would tell me. "The best way to get along with either is to learn all you can, then do your best and don't worry—especially over things over which you have no control."[93]

## Mother's Helper

Nimitz's mother, Anna, was a cook at her father-in-law's hotel, and young Chester helped her in the kitchen. When not in the kitchen he usually could be found hiding behind the bar in the saloon, listening to his grandfather tell stories to customers.

In 1890 Anna married William Nimitz, older brother of her late husband, and the family moved to the nearby town of Kerrville where William managed a small hotel owned by an older sister. As he had in Fredericksburg, Chester helped his mother in the kitchen.

When Nimitz was fifteen, he began working in the hotel on a salaried basis, split-

*Chester W. Nimitz had a relaxed, cheerful disposition that masked his firm determination to defeat the Japanese in World War II.*

ting logs and kindling to keep fireplace wood boxes full, cleaning out stoves and fireplaces, tending the grounds and raking leaves, and working the front desk at night. For these duties he was given room and meals and was paid $15 per month, which he used to buy clothes and textbooks.

Nimitz might well have remained in the Texas Hill Country as a hotel keeper, but he had inherited a wanderlust from his grandfather. He wanted to see the world, but he wasn't sure how to go about it. He admired the "drummers," as the traveling salesmen who frequented the hotel were called, but he didn't think he'd be very good at selling. When he was a junior in high school, a team of surveyors staying at the hotel offered to take him on as an apprentice when he finished school.

Nimitz seriously considered the offer, but the direction of his life was changed that spring when two young army lieutenants registered at the hotel. They told Nimitz about the United States Military Academy at West Point, New York, and how he might go about seeking an appointment.

Nimitz wrote to his congressman, James Slaydon of San Antonio, but all Slaydon's appointments to West Point were taken. Nimitz was asked if he would consider the Naval Academy instead. Although he had never heard of the Naval Academy, he agreed. He excelled on the entrance examination and went to Annapolis in September 1901. His grandfather celebrated by throwing a huge *Wurstfest*, a party featuring German sausages and beer, at his hotel.

## At Annapolis

Although he had not yet finished high school when he entered the Naval Academy, Nimitz was among the academic

---

## The Texas Picnic

Nimitz was extraordinarily proud of his Texas roots. He loved to ask men if they were from Texas, but said he wanted to make sure beforehand so they wouldn't be embarrassed if they weren't.

In 1943, in the middle of the planning of the invasion of the Gilbert and Marshall Islands, Nimitz decided to throw a picnic in Honolulu's Moana Park for all soldiers, sailors, and civilian workers from Texas. About forty thousand showed up to eat barbecue and drink beer with their admiral.

At one point in the festivities, Nimitz climbed onto a stage and made a speech, this excerpt of which is found in *Admiral of the Hills* by Frank Driskill and Dede Casad:

As Texans I know each of you is devoted to our cause and determined to give your best until we accomplish the long hard job necessary to bring about the unconditional surrender of Japan. I say it will be a hard job

because if there's one place larger than Texas it's the Pacific Ocean. . . . Now, more than ever, the eyes of Texas are upon you. I am sure the deeds of her sons and daughters in future months will measure up to the high mark already made: indeed, that this record will be surpassed, and that you will not be so very much older before you will be able to march triumphantly back to Houston . . . or wherever your home may be in Texas, and there receive the well-earned praise of the grateful citizens of Texas and of your country and there await the call for the next Roundup.

The next day, city workers cleaned up the park, picking up an estimated twelve thousand beer bottles to say nothing of plates, utensils, and even a few uniform shirts. Some said more damage was done to Honolulu by the Texas Picnic than by the Japanese raid on December 7, 1941.

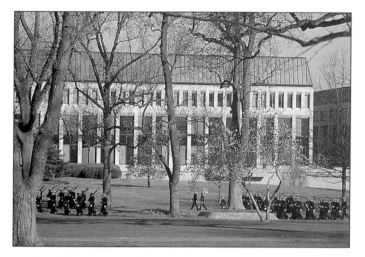

Cadets drill at the Naval Academy in Annapolis, where Nimitz excelled in academics and seamanship.

leaders in his class. And even though his only previous experience on water had been in a rowboat on the Pedernales River flowing through Fredericksburg, he also excelled in seamanship. He graduated in January 1905, nineteen years old and seventh in a class of 114.

His first station was aboard the battleship *Ohio* in the Pacific. One port of call was Tokyo, Japan, at the time that the Japanese were celebrating the naval victory over the Russian fleet at Port Arthur. On a whim at a garden party, Nimitz and a group of fellow midshipmen invited the victorious admiral, Heihachiro Togo, to join them. To their surprise and pleasure he did, drinking a glass of champagne and describing the battle to them. Togo's friendliness and courtesy made a deep impression on Nimitz, and although he would fight the Japanese later, he respected them as men of honor and brother officers.

He received his first command assignment, the gunboat *Panay*, in 1907, and a year later took over the destroyer *Decatur*, one of the youngest destroyer captains in navy history. As he increased in rank and responsibility, Nimitz demonstrated a knack at getting along with people and making them feel comfortable—everyone from Secretary of War and future U.S. president William Howard Taft, to whom he was assigned as an escort in the Philippine Islands, to enlisted men working to repair the *Decatur*.

In 1911, while overseeing the installation of diesel engines in submarines in Quincy, Massachusetts, he met Catherine Freeman, daughter of a wealthy businessman. They were married two years later and would have four children, including Chester Nimitz Jr., who would follow in his father's footsteps as a naval officer.

It was during his time in Quincy that Nimitz, while taking the submarine *Skipjack* on a trial run, dived into a choppy sea to rescue a sailor who had fallen overboard. He received a Silver Lifesaving Medal, which he always wore in a prominent position among all his other decorations. He once told his wife that the medal was special to him since it was earned by saving a life rather than helping to take lives in combat.

## A Key Assignment

Nimitz's assignments included everything from commanding a submarine to establishing a Naval Reserve Officer's Training Corps program at the University of California. In 1935 he was promoted to rear admiral and given command of a battleship division. One of his key assignments was in 1939 as chief of the navy's Bureau of Navigation, the office responsible for making personnel assignments. With war imminent, more men were being promoted into top commands. Nimitz frequently was summoned by President Franklin Roosevelt and asked for his evaluation of his brother officers. Roosevelt grew to respect and depend on Nimitz's judgment.

So highly was Nimitz regarded by Roosevelt that early in 1941 he was offered the post of commander in chief, U.S. fleet, second only to the chief of naval operations. Had he accepted, he would have leapfrogged more than fifty admirals senior to him. Nimitz, however, declined, claiming he was too junior for such an appointment.

The refusal turned out to be the most fortunate decision of his career. Instead of Nimitz, Admiral Husband Kimmel, a good friend, was appointed. Therefore, when the Japanese attack on Pearl Harbor on December 7 left much of the U.S. fleet in ruins, it was Kimmel's career, not Nimitz's, that was in ruins, as well.

A week after Pearl Harbor, Secretary of the Navy Frank Knox was in the White House. "Tell Nimitz," Roosevelt shouted, "to get the hell out to Pearl and stay there till the war is won."[94] This time, there was no way for Nimitz to refuse. When he told his wife, she congratulated him on his appointment to what she thought was a mighty fleet. "Darling," he told her, "the fleet's at the bottom of the sea. Nobody must know that here, but I've got to tell you."[95]

## An Expression of Loyalty

When he was a young officer, Chester Nimitz became one of the U.S. Navy's leading experts on diesel engines. Before World War I, he was assigned to Germany to study the manufacture, installation, and maintenance of such engines in submarines. After the war broke out, and with American submarines requiring new and better diesels, a representative of a St. Louis company called on Nimitz in his Brooklyn Navy Yard office. Lieutenant Walter Anderson, who had the desk next to Nimitz, recalled the conversation. The quotation is from *Nimitz* by E. B. Potter.

> Finally it became plain that they wanted to employ Nimitz. This would of course have meant his resignation from the Navy. The man made Nimitz a definite offer of $25,000 a year and a five-year contract. [Nimitz's pay at this time was $3,458 per year.] . . . Knowing how valuable Nimitz was to the Navy, I was gravely disturbed, but to my great relief Nimitz slowly replied, "No, thank you, I do not want to leave the Navy." That was indeed wonderful to hear. There was some more talk, and the man became more persuasive: "At any rate, money is no obstacle to us. Write your own ticket." . . . After a brief pause Nimitz reiterated, "No, I don't want to leave the Navy." The man from St. Louis departed. I rushed over to Nimitz and said, "Chester, I couldn't help hearing what went on. I'm the only one here to represent the Navy. That was wonderful of you. Thank God you refused that offer. We need you!"

The battleship USS West Virginia *burns as it settles to the bottom of Pearl Harbor. Nimitz was shocked by what he saw when he assumed command of the Pacific Fleet.*

It was Christmas Day when Nimitz arrived in Pearl Harbor. Climbing from his seaplane into a boat for the short ride to shore, he was shocked at what he saw and smelled—sunken ships of which only the topmasts were visible, others heavily damaged; the odor of charred wood and rotting bodies. "A terrible sight,"[96] he said to one of the welcoming officers.

## On the Treadmill

Soon he was far too busy to dwell on the tragedy that had overtaken his navy. He had to deal with refitting damaged ships, replacing personnel—all while taking precautions against another attack. "To me it seems like I am on a treadmill," he wrote to Catherine, "whirling around actively but not getting anywhere very fast."[97]

The damage to morale was almost as great as the damage to ships. The Pacific Fleet included some of the most capable officers in the navy, many of whom thought their careers would be ended by the Pearl Harbor debacle. Nimitz knew these men

66

would be valuable to the war effort. At his first staff meeting, he surprised them by saying, "Certain key members of the staff I insist I want to keep."[98] Furthermore, he said, his plan was to go on the attack as soon as possible. Spirits soared.

His immediate task was to hold the line between Hawaii and Midway Island and to keep the sea lanes open between the West Coast and Australia. And yet, a "holding" war wasn't enough. The United States had been hit hard and needed to hit back. The first major opportunity came in April 1942, when intelligence sources forecast a move by the Japanese into the Coral Sea toward Australia and New Guinea.

Nimitz faced a decision. His most able commander, Admiral William F. "Bull" Halsey, and two of his aircraft carriers were on another mission, but he had to gamble, sending his remaining carriers, the *Yorktown* and *Lexington*, to stop the Japanese advance.

Even though the *Lexington* was sunk and the carrier *Yorktown* severely damaged, the Japanese also suffered heavy losses and the assault on New Guinea was averted. The Japanese had been turned back for the first time in the war.

Their invasion plans thwarted, the Japanese were bound to seek another target. Nimitz studied the map and chose Midway Island, the westernmost American stronghold, as the most likely choice. He predicted that his rival, Japanese admiral Yamamoto Isoroku, would not bypass the island, thus leaving an American force at his rear.

Even before the Coral Sea battle, Nimitz went to Midway to assess the island's defenses. He asked U.S. Marine lieutenant colonel Harold Shannon what he needed to withstand a Japanese invasion. When Shannon responded with a long list, Nimitz asked, "If I get you all these things you say you need, then can you hold Midway against a major amphibious assault?"[99] Yes, he could, Shannon answered. Nimitz smiled and seemed to relax.

## Battle of Midway

His intent, however, was that no Japanese ground troops would have the chance to come ashore at Midway. "This time we will not wait for Yamamoto," he said. "We are going to strike first."[100]

Midway was even more of a gamble than the Coral Sea. Against four Japanese carriers and a large supporting force, Nimitz could send only the carriers *Enterprise*, *Hornet*, and *Yorktown*, the last hastily patched up after being torpedoed in the Coral Sea. The battle group, Task Force 16, was commanded by Admiral Raymond Spruance.

The battle was fought June 4–6, 1942. Nimitz, in Pearl Harbor, gave Spruance only a few instructions. He always preferred to let his officers on the scene fight the battles. "Horses pull harder when the reins lie loose,"[101] he liked to say. Consequently, he spent most of the battle listening to radio transmissions and receiving messages.

The Battle of Midway was the turning point in the Pacific war. The Japanese lost four carriers and, lacking the industrial capacity to replace them, were never again able to mount a major invasion. In his communiqué after the battle, Nimitz recognized the importance of the victory but couldn't resist adding one of his infamous puns:

> Pearl Harbor has now been partially avenged. Vengeance will not be complete until Japanese sea power is reduced to impotence. We have made substantial progress in that direction. Perhaps we will be forgiven if we claim that we are about midway to that objective.[102]

Two U.S. Navy dive-bombers fly over a burning enemy carrier during the Battle of Midway. The American victory halted the Japanese advance across the Pacific.

The Japanese were wounded but nowhere near impotent. Balked in the Central Pacific, they pushed south. On July 6 they landed troops on Guadalcanal, chief island in the southern Solomons, and began to build an airfield. Nimitz and the Allies could not afford to let the enemy have a base so close to Australia, and on August 7 the First Marine Division was put ashore. After heavy fighting, the marines captured the airfield. The Japanese sent reinforcements, and soon the Americans were desperately defending a small piece of land surrounding the airfield.

Nimitz had to take drastic action. He went to Guadalcanal to take a look for himself. He asked the marine commander, Archer Vandegrift, "Are you going to hold this beachhead, General? Are you going to stay here?"

"Hell, yes," Vandegrift replied. "Why not?"[103]

Nimitz knew he needed a more aggressive man in charge of the naval operation. Reluctantly, he relieved his old friend Robert Ghormley, with whom he had been a midshipman at Annapolis, and replaced him with Halsey. The Japanese were beaten back in their attempts to reinforce Guadalcanal and finally, in February 1943, evacuated their remaining troops from the island.

## Presidential Decision

The Allies now were on the offensive. The questions were where would the next offensive take place and who would lead it. General Douglas MacArthur wanted a march up the New Guinea coast, to be followed by an invasion of the Philippine Islands, and then northward to Japan. Nimitz and the navy favored a drive across the Central Pacific, "hopping" from island to island, building air bases on each to support the next jump. At last President Roosevelt decided that both strategies would be employed.

In November Nimitz launched his Central Pacific offensive with an invasion of Tarawa and Makin in the Gilbert Islands. Makin fell easily, but the Japanese had heavily fortified Tarawa, and more than a thousand Marines were killed.

Nimitz was disturbed by the heavy losses. Despite protests from his staff, he went to Tarawa before it was secured to see what had gone wrong. As he walked along the beach, bodies were still washing ashore. "It's the first time I've smelled death,"[104] Nimitz murmured. He could see, however, that the naval bombardment preceding the invasion had done little to eliminate the Japanese fortifications. Precise bombing by aircraft was the answer—an answer that would result in fewer casualties in other invasions.

As the offensive across the Pacific continued, another dispute with MacArthur arose. The navy proposed to bypass the Philippines and attack the island of Formosa. MacArthur, commander in the Philippines when they fell to the Japanese in early 1942, was furious. Again Roosevelt had to be called in. At a face-to-face meeting in Hawaii in July, both Nimitz and MacArthur argued for their plans. MacArthur won out, and Nimitz agreed to give naval support to the invasion of the Philippines.

The invasion would be supported by the Third Fleet, commanded by Halsey, whose orders from Nimitz included the wording: "You are always free to make local decisions in connection with the handling of forces under your command."[105] The Japanese, counting on Halsey's combative nature, devised a plan to lure him away from the island of Leyte, where the Americans had landed. With Halsey's ships gone, two other fleets were to rush through the unprotected San Bernadino and Surigao Straits and shell the vulnerable American troops on shore.

## Tremendous Cost of Victory

The plan almost worked, but luckily for the Americans on shore, the few ships left by Halsey fought bravely against heavy odds. After a three-hour battle, the Japanese commander withdrew.

The Americans had been fortunate to avoid a serious defeat, and Halsey was saved from a likely court-martial. Nimitz would never have criticized Halsey for his blunder, but he made this frank assessment in a top-secret letter to Chief of Naval Operations Ernest King: "It never occurred to me that Halsey, knowing the composition of the [Japanese] ships . . . would leave San Bernadino Strait unguarded."[106]

Meanwhile the Central Pacific offensive continued. The conquest of the Gilberts was followed by an assault on the Marshall Islands in January 1944, and on Saipan in the Mariana Islands in June. The capture of Saipan was critical since the airbase built there was within B-29 range of Tokyo. An even closer base was possible after the capture of the island of Iwo Jima in February 1945.

All these victories, however, were won at tremendous cost. More than 4,500 Americans were killed in the Marianas and 6,000 more on Iwo Jima. Some American newspapers, noting that MacArthur had lost far fewer troops on New Guinea and in the Philippines, blamed Nimitz for poor tactics. These attacks deeply wounded the admiral, as did accusing letters from relatives of the slain.

*Nimitz agreed to support MacArthur's return to the Philippines with the Third Fleet (pictured). The operation nearly ended in disaster.*

Nimitz abhorred loss of life. He knew that death in war was inevitable but would never, like Halsey, publicly pronounce that his strategy was "Kill Japs. Kill Japs. Kill more Japs."[107] It was not surprising, therefore, that when informed in February 1945 that an atomic bomb would be ready for use against Japan in August, he pondered the devastating effect on Japan. "You know," he told the messenger who brought the top-secret document, "I guess I was just born a few years too soon."[108]

Soon after two atomic bombs were dropped in August, the Japanese capitulated. President Harry Truman, who had succeeded Roosevelt on the latter's death in April, announced that MacArthur would formally, as supreme commander, accept the surrender for the Allies, an appointment that did not sit well with the navy. "Well, this does it,"[109] muttered the usually placid Nimitz.

## Surrender on the *Missouri*

So great was the navy's grumbling that a compromise was reached. The surrender would take place on Nimitz's flagship, the battleship *Missouri*, and Nimitz would accept the surrender on behalf of the United States. After the ceremony, Nimitz released a statement:

> On board all naval vessels at sea and in port, and at our many island bases in the Pacific, there is rejoicing and thanksgiving. The long and bitter struggle . . . is at an end. . . . Now we turn to the great

*On board his flagship, the battleship USS Missouri, Nimitz accepts the Japanese surrender on behalf of the United States. As part of a compromise, MacArthur accepted for the Allies.*

tasks of reconstruction and restoration. I am confident that we will be able to apply the same skill, resourcefulness and keen thinking to these problems as were applied to the problems of winning the victory.[110]

Nimitz was not colorful. He did not, as he once said of MacArthur, "make Jovian pronouncements complete with thunderbolts."[111] A modest man, he was one of the few top commanders in World War II who never wrote his memoirs. And yet, as a biographer, Edwin Hoyt, wrote, "Halsey was the man to win a battle for you, Spruance was the man to win a campaign, but Nimitz was the man to win a war."[112]

# Chapter 7

# Eisenhower: Conqueror of Europe

**D**wight Eisenhower was as much of a politician during World War II as a soldier. Besides having to make war on the Germans, "Ike" had to keep peace among his American generals, between his generals and the British, between the British and American generals and the French, among the various factions of the French, and finally between the Russians and everyone. His task was to defeat Nazi Germany while, at the same time, dealing with such diverse and demanding personalities as Franklin Roosevelt, Charles de Gaulle, Winston Churchill, and Joseph Stalin. With this kind of political experience, there's little wonder that, after the war, he was twice elected president of the United States.

There was little in his background to suggest a military career. His parents were members of the River Brethren, a strict religious sect that preached pacifism. His father had tried and abandoned farming, failed as a storekeeper in Abilene, Kansas, and finally took a job as a railroad mechanic in Deni-

son, Texas. It was there, on October 14, 1890, that Dwight, the third of seven brothers, was born. Two years later the family moved back to Abilene, where Eisenhower's father worked for a creamery.

The Eisenhower family was literally from the wrong side of the tracks. The railroad that divided working-class south Abilene from the wealthier north side ran right in front of their house. Despite their parents' beliefs, the Eisenhower boys often fought—with each other or with town bullies who mocked them because of their poverty.

Every member of the Eisenhower family worked. None of the children received an allowance, but each was assigned a small plot of land behind the family home. In these gardens, Dwight and his brothers raised vegetables that they sold for spending money. Dwight sold corn in order to buy football equipment.

Football was a big part of Eisenhower's life. He was a star athlete in high school, but

*Dwight Eisenhower was as well versed in politics as he was in warfare, having had to remind the Allies that their enemies were the Germans, not each other.*

nothing special in the classroom, as one of his teachers described, "At times he was slow in comprehension almost to the point of denseness."[113]

## Navy, Then Army

After graduating from high school in 1909, Eisenhower went to work in the same creamery where his father was employed, earning money to help his brother Edgar through law school. The plan was that Edgar would then put Dwight through, but Uncle Sam paid the way, instead. A friend gave him the idea of going to the U.S. Naval Academy.

Eisenhower had no interest in a military career, but considerable interest in a free college education. He studied hard, even returning to high school for refresher courses, and surprised himself by doing well on the examination. He was bitterly disappointed, however, to discover that he was too old for the Naval Academy.

Eisenhower returned to work at the creamery, determined to try to save enough money—with some help from Edgar—for college. Then he learned that West Point, unlike Annapolis, had no age limit. He easily passed the West Point exam and was accepted early in 1911.

When he took the oath of allegiance as a cadet, Eisenhower's outlook changed. He was overcome with a sense of duty and patriotism. Later, he wrote:

Whatever had gone before, this was a supreme moment. . . . A feeling came over me that the expression "The United States of America" would now and henceforth mean something different than it ever had before. From here on in it would be the nation I would be serving, not myself. Suddenly the flag meant something. . . . Across half a century, I can look back and see a rawboned, gawky Kansas boy from the farm country, earnestly repeating the words that would make him a cadet.[114]

Eisenhower's record at West Point was much the same as in high school. Academically, he was in the bottom half of his class. In conduct, he was near the bottom, his sense of fun constantly getting him in trouble with upperclassmen and officers. Once as a "plebe," or freshman, he was ordered by a senior to appear for inspection in "full-dress coat," or formal dress. Eisenhower decided to take the order literally and appeared dressed in his uniform coat and nothing else.

## A Popular Cadet

Personally, Eisenhower was one of the most popular cadets, with his wide grin and warm, open manner. Everyone liked "Ike." Athletically, he excelled until suffering a serious knee injury in football. The injury was so serious that it almost prevented him from earning a commission in the army.

He graduated in 1915, and his first assignment was in San Antonio, Texas. In October he met Mamie Doud, the nineteen-year-old daughter of a wealthy Colorado family that spent winters in Texas. On Valentine's Day 1916 they were married.

A year later the United States was at war, but while brother officers were making names for themselves in France, Eisenhower was stuck at home. He proved to be so valuable as a training officer that his commander would not release him for a battlefield assignment. When his orders to France finally came through, World War I had been over for a week.

His next assignment was as an aide to General Fox Conner, commander of the Panama Canal Zone. Conner saw great potential in Eisenhower and arranged for him to attend the Command and General Staff School at Fort Leavenworth, Kansas, a grooming point for future generals. Eisenhower led his class and was clearly headed for great things.

After several diverse assignments, in 1934 Eisenhower became assistant to Chief of Staff Douglas MacArthur. When MacArthur left active duty to set up defense forces in the Philippine Islands, then a U.S. possession, Eisenhower accompanied him

*Eisenhower met his wife, Mamie Doud, during his first military assignment in San Antonio, Texas. They were married on Valentine's Day.*

## Ike the Young Leader

Much to his disappointment, Eisenhower spent World War I in the United States. While the young captain desperately wanted to join the fighting in France, he was considered so valuable as a training officer by his commander that he was kept behind. His talent as a motivator, so evident during World War II, was recorded in a letter written by a trainee, Edward Thayer, and reprinted in *Ike the Soldier* by Merle Miller:

> Our new captain, Eisenhower by name, is, I believe, one of the most efficient and best Army officers in the country. . . . He is a corker and has put more fight into us in three days than we got in all the previous time we were here. He is a giant for build and at West Point was a noted football player and physical culture fiend. He knows his job, is enthusiastic, can tell us what he wants us to do, and is pretty human, though wickedly harsh and abrupt. He has given us wonderful bayonet drills. He gets the fellows' imaginations worked up and hollers and yells and makes us shout and stomp until we go tearing into the air as if we mean business. . . . Eisenhower kept sending different ones of us up to the sentries with all kinds of answers to their challenges, to see if they know how to handle the situation. The rest of us stood around and laughed and smoked. Every now and then Eisenhower would jump on us and say we were having too good a time, call us to attention and put us through the manual [of arms] for five minutes . . . but you could see that he enjoyed it all too.

—on leave from the army but retaining his rank of lieutenant colonel.

Eisenhower's great talent was getting along with people—even the pompous, overbearing MacArthur. He had great respect for MacArthur as a soldier but privately thought his egotistical behavior ridiculous, calling him "General Impossible" in his diary.

It was not until early 1940 that Eisenhower was able to resume his army career. Five days after the attack on Pearl Harbor, he received a call from a friend in the War Department in Washington, D.C. "The Chief says for you to hop on a plane and get up here right away," he was told. "Tell your boss that your formal orders will come through later."[115] The "Chief" was General George C. Marshall, army chief of staff.

Years before, Conner had recommended Eisenhower to Marshall, who now wanted Eisenhower's view of Japan's attack on the Philippines.

### A Big Assignment

Eisenhower's frank reply—that the Philippines could not be defended—impressed Marshall, and Eisenhower was made deputy chief of the War Plans Division with the temporary rank of brigadier general. He was afraid he might again be stuck at home when his colleagues were fighting, but it was only six months until he found out otherwise.

Eisenhower had worked on an ambitious plan for an invasion of France across the English Channel later in 1942. He took it to Marshall, recommending that the chief

*Eisenhower shares a lighter moment with Army Chief of Staff George C. Marshall. One of Eisenhower's greatest talents was his ability to get along with people.*

of staff read it thoroughly. "His reply still lives in my memory," Eisenhower wrote later. "'I certainly do want to read it. You may be the man who executes it. If that's the case, when can you leave?'"[116]

Although Eisenhower promptly went to London, the invasion did not take place. The British did not think there was enough time, men, or material to attempt a cross-channel invasion. British general Ian Jacob summed up their feelings: "A landing in Northern France was the accepted goal of the Anglo-American strategy, but nothing would have been more fatal to the Allied cause than an unsuccessful attempt."[117]

Still, something needed to be done. The Germans had invaded and were advancing rapidly through the Soviet Union. The Al-

lies knew that if they did not go on the offensive somewhere and draw away German strength, the Soviet Union might crumble. The place chosen was North Africa.

The invasion of North Africa, nicknamed Operation Torch, was nowhere near the size of the projected invasion of France. President Franklin Roosevelt and Marshall decided that Eisenhower would not only plan but also command the invasion—both American and British troops.

The reason for having an American in overall command was that much of the territory involved was French. Eisenhower hoped to persuade the supposedly neutral French of Morocco and Algeria to fight with them against the Germans. To do so, he needed to enlist the help of an influential French leader to convince his countrymen. He chose General Henri Giraud, who, on arriving at Eisenhower's headquarters, promptly demanded that full command of all troops, including Americans, be turned over to him.

## The Darlan Affair

Frustrated, Eisenhower turned to Admiral François Darlan, who made a deal to declare an armistice and bring all his troops and the French navy to the Allies. In the end, however, the French sank their fleet rather than turn it over, the French government repudiated Darlan, and some of the French troops came to the Allies' aid during the invasion while others opposed it.

It was Eisenhower's first, but by no means his last, experience dealing with French politics, and he found it distasteful. He wrote to a friend:

> I think sometimes that I am a cross between a one timer soldier, a pseudo-statesman, a jack-legged politician and a crooked diplomat. I walk a soapy tightrope in a rainstorm with a blazing furnace on one side and a pack of ravenous tigers on the other. If I get across, my greatest public reward would be a quiet little cottage on the side of a slow-moving stream.[118]

Much later, after dealing with the prickly de Gaulle, he said, "I must say that next to the weather they [the French] have caused me more trouble in this war than any other single factor."[119]

The landings themselves—at Casablanca, Oran, and Algiers on November 7–8—had little opposition. Eisenhower was in his headquarters at Gibraltar when his troops landed. He had done everything possible to make the invasion a success. Now, he found out what the last-minute waiting was like:

> During those anxious hours, I first realized, I think, how inexorably and inescapably strain and tension wear away at the leader's endurance, his judgment and his confidence. The pressure becomes more acute because of the duty of a staff constantly to present to the commander the worst side of an eventuality. The seriousness of the possibilities are reflected in the demeanor of the staff members and the commander inherits an additional load in preserving optimism in himself and his command.[120]

## Defeat at the Kasserine Pass

Eisenhower had reason to worry. In February 1943 German general Erwin Rommel, pursued by Montgomery, attacked westward. His battle-hardened Afrika Korps sliced through the green Americans at the Kasserine Pass, and only a heroic defense by a largely British force prevented a major defeat.

*Protected by a smoke screen, American and British troops land on a beach in North Africa. They met little opposition.*

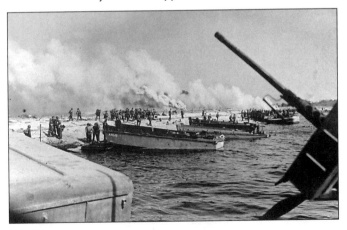

Eisenhower was deeply troubled but determined that the Americans would learn from the experience. "All our people," he wrote Marshall, "from the very highest to the very lowest have learned that this is not a child's game and are ready and eager to get down to the fundamental business of profiting by the lessons they have learned."[121]

He replaced his field commander with an old friend, George Patton, who had as his second in command Eisenhower's West Point classmate General Omar Bradley. "Now," Eisenhower wrote to Marshall, "there will be no more hesitation, no more defensive tactics when attack is needed."[122]

Attack is just what Eisenhower got from the aggressive Patton, and by mid-May all German and Italian troops in North Africa had surrendered. Next the Allies decided to invade Sicily, then Italy, knocking the Italians out of the war. Eisenhower again was placed in command, with Patton and Montgomery as his field commanders.

From now until the end of the war, Eisenhower would have to use all his diplomatic skills to reduce the friction between British and American officers. Montgomery, especially, had little respect for his American counterparts, and they in turn openly considered him vain and too protective of his reputation. Privately, Eisenhower agreed, writing to Marshall, "He is unquestionably able, but very conceited. . . . He is so proud of his successes to date that he will never willingly make a single move until he is absolutely certain of success."[123]

*General George Patton was selected by Eisenhower to be his new field commander after the American defeat at Kasserine Pass.*

## A Mistake in Italy

The conquest of Sicily, begun on July 10, was quick and fairly easy, but Eisenhower, in the opinion of most military historians, had made a mistake by not simultaneously invading the "toe" of boot-shaped Italy opposite Sicily. As it was, two German divisions were able to escape and were saved for later battles against the Allies.

In early September the Allies landed in Italy. The main striking force, the American Fifth Army under General Mark Clark, went ashore at Salerno, south of Naples. It was now that Eisenhower made what has been called his other greatest mistake.

The invasion of Italy led to the fall of dictator Benito Mussolini and to the installation of Pietro Badoglio as prime minister. Eisenhower's plan was that Badoglio should broadcast a surrender and call on Italian troops to support the Allies. With Italian help, paratroopers of the Eighty-second Airborne Division would take the airfields near Rome and the Germans would be caught in the middle.

At the last minute, however, Badoglio's fear of the Germans was too much. He went back on his promises to Eisenhower, who—without assurance of Italian support—called off the attack on Rome. Many military experts think the airborne assault on Rome probably would have succeeded and was well worth the gamble.

At the time, however, Eisenhower was hailed as a hero. There was even talk in the United States of making him a candidate for president in 1944. "Baloney," was his response. "Why can't a simple soldier be left alone to carry out his orders?" [124]

Eisenhower's next orders were to be the most important of all. At a conference in Tehran, Iran, the Soviets' Stalin had been assured that Operation Overlord, the invasion of France, would take place in 1944. At Tehran Stalin pointedly asked Roosevelt

*Stalin, Roosevelt, and British prime minister Winston Churchill meet in Tehran. Stalin wanted assurance that the invasion of France would take place in 1944.*

who would be in command, trying to force a decision in order to forestall another delay by the Allies.

## Supreme Commander

On December 7, 1943, exactly two years after Pearl Harbor, Eisenhower received word that Roosevelt, headed home from Tehran, wanted to meet him in Tunis. The president deplaned, got inside a waiting car with Eisenhower, and said, "Well, Ike, you are going to command Overlord."

"Mr. President," Eisenhower was able to respond, "I realize such an appointment involved a difficult decision. I hope you will not be disappointed." [125]

After a short trip to Washington, Eisenhower arrived in London on January 14, 1944, to prepare for Overlord. Eisenhower decided that he would retain overall command until the troops were ashore. Command would then pass to Montgomery until Eisenhower could move his headquarters to France, whereupon he would take command once more.

This plan did not sit well with General Alan Brooke, who was General Marshall's British counterpart, or with Montgomery, who had previously written in his diary that Eisenhower "knows practically nothing about how to make war, and definitely nothing about how to fight battles." [126] Both tried to convince Churchill to make Montgomery commander in France. When Churchill mentioned the possibility to Eisenhower, the American commander threatened to quit and return to the United States. Churchill quickly backed down.

Eisenhower worked long days and many nights getting Overlord ready. Tanks and airplanes by the thousands and soldiers by the millions flooded into Britain. "I must admit that sometimes I feel a thousand years old when I struggle to my bed at night," [127] he wrote.

Finally, everything was ready. The tides would be favorable on June 5, 6, and 7. Troops were loaded aboard ships, but rain and high winds made sailing impossible. Eisenhower waited. The next favorable tide would not be for almost two weeks. Finally, his meteorologists reported a break in the weather. A calm sea was predicted for Tuesday, June 6. Before dawn on June 5, Eisenhower met with his top staff. Some urged invasion; others, caution. Eisenhower was briefly silent and then said, "O.K., we'll go." [128]

## A Lonely Commander

The first troops to head for France were those of the Eighty-second Airborne Division, who would land behind German lines. Eisenhower went to their base to see them off. His air commander had predicted that up to 75 percent would be killed. Eisenhower saluted each plane as it took off. Afterward his driver recalled, "General Eisenhower turned, shoulders sagging, the loneliest man in the world." [129]

To Eisenhower's great relief, the casualty figures were far better than expected, both among the paratroops and those land-

*Eisenhower gives encouragement to the first troops to head for France, the paratroopers of the Eighty-second Airborne division.*

ing on the beaches. Only on Omaha Beach, where the American First Army under Bradley came under heavy fire, was the toll high.

Once the Allies established a beach-head, however, they had trouble breaking through the German defenses. Montgomery, especially, was bogged down trying to take the city of Caen. Despite all attempts to "get Monty on his bicycle and start moving,"[130] the British general was cautious. Eisenhower even considered replacing him but knew, as British author Max Hastings later wrote, that Montgomery could not be fired "without inflicting an intolerable blow to British national confidence."[131]

Eisenhower turned once more to Patton and his Third Army. The breakout was

finally achieved. By November the Allied front had pushed eastward 350 miles. The next month, however, the Germans surprised Eisenhower with a massive counterattack. They pushed a portion of the Allied line back fifty miles in what became known as the Battle of the Bulge.

Eisenhower quickly demonstrated his skill as a battlefield commander. By mid-January the Allied line had been restored. Sir Arthur Bryant, in a biography of Brooke, wrote, "Nor in the hour of crisis was the Supreme Commander unworthy of the men he led. Calamity acted on Eisenhower like a restorative and brought out all the greatness in his character."[132]

The Battle of the Bulge was the German army's last gasp. It retreated through the spring of 1945 while Eisenhower's troops advanced to the Rhine, crossing at Remagen on March 7. Two months later it was all over. On May 7 German general Alfred Jodl came to Eisenhower's headquarters, a plain red schoolhouse in Reims, to surrender. Eisenhower refused to see him, letting his aide, General Bedell Smith, sign the document.

## Message of Victory

Then the man who a little more than three years earlier had been an obscure lieutenant colonel and who now wore five stars on his shoulders dictated a simple message: "The mission of this Allied force was fulfilled at 0241, local time, May 7, 1945."[133]

## His View of the Enemy

Warfare to Eisenhower was a deadly serious business. His first duty, he thought, was to his country and the men serving under him, not to the military profession. Others might observe the traditions and formalities of the distant past, when war was almost a gentleman's game, but not Eisenhower, as he wrote in *In Review:*

> When [German General Jürgen] von Armin was brought through Algiers on his way to captivity, some members of my staff felt that I should observe the custom of bygone days and allow him to call on me. The tradition that all professional soldiers are really comrades in arms has, in tattered form, persisted to this day. For me, World War II was far too personal a thing to entertain such feelings. Daily as it progressed there grew within me the conviction that as never before in a war between many nations the forces that stood for human good and men's rights were this time confronted by a completely evil conspiracy with which no compromise could be tolerated. Because only by the utter destruction of the Axis [Germany, Italy, and Japan] was a decent world possible, the war became for me a crusade in the traditional sense of that often misused word. In this specific instance, I told my Intelligence officer to get any information he possibly could out of the captured generals but that, as far as I was concerned, I was interested only in those who were not yet captured.

Dwight Eisenhower would go on to other great things, but this is the achievement for which he is best remembered. Biographer and military historian E. K. G. Sixsmith summed up:

> We are left with the picture of a commander of manifest integrity who warmed the heart and uplifted the spirit of everyone who worked with him. His special genius was his skill at management. He managed the generals, the admirals and the air marshals, and even the politicians. . . . His own heart and mind were with the fighting man and his preference would have been to be in command of the forefront of the battle. But that was not to be his destiny. . . . His task was to weld together a force which was not only an Allied force but one drawn from all Services, and to direct it so that its whole weight was used most effectively to the single aim of the defeat of the common enemy. That he did superbly.[134]

# Chapter 8

# Montgomery: A Study in Contrasts

ield Marshal Bernard Law Montgomery was a man of contradictions. His British countrymen hailed him as a hero, and he was idolized by the ordinary soldiers he commanded. At the same time, he was disliked and distrusted by many of his fellow commanders. His superior, American Dwight Eisenhower, said that Montgomery was "a good man to serve under; a difficult man to serve with; and an impossible man to serve over."[135] His own prime minister, Winston Churchill, once called him "a little man on the make."[136]

He unquestionably had a brilliant grasp of military strategy but had trouble putting strategies into practice. He won great victories, but they were not as great as they could have been. While some military historians have called him one of history's most gifted commanders, others, like Martin Blumenson, have labeled him "the most over-rated general of World War II."[137]

"Monty" was born in 1887, the fifth child of nine children of an Anglican clergyman who had at age thirty-four married Maud Farrar, a girl of sixteen. He was less than two years old when his father

*Bernard Law Montgomery was hailed by his countrymen, idolized by his soldiers, and disliked by his fellow commanders.*

was appointed Anglican bishop of Tasmania, an island near Australia, and the family moved halfway around the world.

His mild-mannered father was away from home much of the time on church business and left the raising of the children and the running of the household to his strong-willed young wife, who accomplished both tasks efficiently but "with an absence of affectionate understanding."[138] The children rose at dawn, cleaned their rooms, shined their shoes, and chopped kindling. A half hour of lessons, room inspection, and prayers followed. Only then was breakfast served.

Despite Bishop Montgomery's position in the church, the family was far from wealthy, mainly because he donated so much of his own salary to church work. The younger children wore hand-me-down clothes, and the bishop's wife was once described as the worst-dressed woman on Tasmania.

## A Difficult Child

Living far from home in meager circumstances, Maud Montgomery seemed to take out her own unhappiness on her children, especially Bernard. And Bernard, by his own admission, was the most difficult of the children. His mother's routine instructions to the others were to "go find out what Bernard's doing and tell him to stop it."[139] At a birthday party he loudly referred to his hostess as an "old sow." He once chased a playmate through the house with a carving knife. Often after committing some misdeed, he would be asked by his father to join in a prayer for guidance even as his mother waited outside the room with a stick to beat him.

In 1901 Bishop Montgomery was ordered to London for a new assignment. On the family's return, Bernard was enrolled in St. Paul's School, where, to his parents' dismay, he chose to be in the "army" class designed for those set on a military career. His mother was especially disturbed, which may well have been why Montgomery made the decision and probably made him all the more determined to follow it.

He was an excellent athlete but a below-average student. Only when a teacher warned him that his grades would have to improve if he hoped to enter the Royal Military College at Sandhurst did Montgomery apply himself to his studies. His conduct—effective when placed in a leadership role but rebellious when given orders—was a foretaste of his military career.

Montgomery enrolled in Sandhurst early in 1907. Although he excelled in sports, his brashness and air of self-importance won him few friends. He became the leader of a small group of cadets who terrorized their classmates. He was almost expelled when he set a classmate's shirttails on fire and the victim suffered serious burns.

Cadets usually graduated from Sandhurst after just one year. Although Montgomery's grades were good, his conduct had been such that he was told he would require

*At the Royal Military College at Sandhurst (pictured), Montgomery's brazen behavior earned him few friends and an extra six months of study.*

an extra six months. Shocked and disappointed, he began to take his work more seriously.

## Learning to Soldier

On his commissioning as a second lieutenant, he joined the Royal Warwickshire Regiment, which was shortly thereafter sent to India. Montgomery threw himself wholeheartedly into soldiering. He worked hard to improve his horsemanship and learned Hindustani languages to communicate better with the native soldiers. A fellow officer remembered that he "entered into all these activities with zest and keenness." [140] So keen was he that his colleagues found him rather boring. "For two months I had to sit next to this fellow at dinner," one said, "and all he could talk about was the army." [141]

The regiment was posted back to England in 1912, and World War I erupted two years later. Montgomery showed exceptional bravery in an assault on a German position at the village of Meteren but was wounded so severely that a grave was dug for him. He recovered, was decorated with the Distinguished Service Order and promoted to captain, and returned to France. By the time the war ended he was already, at age thirty, a lieutenant colonel.

Montgomery learned valuable lessons during World War I. The first was the necessity of planning. He condemned what he considered the needless waste of men's lives in blind headlong charges. He wrote of an order to attack given with

no reconnaissance, no plan, no covering fire. We rushed up the hill, came under heavy fire, my Company Commander was wounded and there were many casualties. Nobody knew what to do, so we returned to the original position from which we had begun to attack. If this was real war it struck me as most curious and did not seem to make any sense against the background of what I had been reading. [142]

Thereafter, he made it a rule as a commander to plan thoroughly—far too slowly, some thought—before committing his troops to action.

## Becoming a Leader

The other lesson Montgomery learned was that soldiers respond better to commands when they know their commander. "There was little contact between the generals and the soldiers," he wrote later. "The higher staff were out of touch with the regimental officers and with the troops."[143] When he became a general, he made it a point to circulate among his troops, something considered mere showmanship by some of his colleagues.

Between the wars Montgomery had several diverse assignments. He attended the prestigious Staff College and served in Ireland during the uprisings of 1920–1922. He was appointed to head a committee to rewrite the army's manual on infantry training. When the committee disagreed with his views, Montgomery simply dismissed the committee and wrote the final version himself. He bragged that "it was considered excellent, especially by the author."[144]

Montgomery went abroad again, first commanding a battalion in Palestine and then a regiment in Egypt, where he nearly caused a revolt by denying his men the pleasures of nearby Alexandria; he also laid down regulations that interfered with their private lives and inflicted harsh punishment for minor offenses. Fortunately for Montgomery, his superior officers stepped in and convinced him to ease up before he lost control and fatally damaged his career. He was "definitely above the average rank," one general wrote, and should attain high rank unless

"a certain high-handedness . . . becomes too pronounced."[145]

It was shortly before his assignment in Palestine that Montgomery fell deeply in love for the first and only time in his life. In 1926, while on a skiing trip in Switzerland,

## On Leadership

While many experts may be critical of Bernard Montgomery's tactics and his lack of cooperation with superior officers, all agree that he was a superb leader. The men who served under him in North Africa, Sicily, Italy, and after the invasion of France adored him.

He was not easy on his troops. Indeed, he insisted on rigorous drills and soldiers' being in excellent physical condition. But, even though he was a demanding officer, he instilled in his troops a confidence in him and in themselves. His view of leadership was expressed in this excerpt from an infantry training manual he wrote in 1930 that appears in *Montgomery of Alamein* by Alun Chalfont:

> Leadership depends on simple and straightforward human qualities. A leader, above all, must have the confidence of his men. He will gain their confidence by commanding their respect—respect for his determination and ready acceptance of responsibility; for the clearness and simplicity of his orders and the firm way in which he insists that they shall be carried out; for his thorough knowledge of his profession; for his sense of justice; for his common sense; for his keenness, energy and habit of forethought; for his sense of humour; for his indifference to personal danger and the readiness with which he shares his men's hardships; and his persistent good humour in the face of difficulties; and for the obvious pride he takes in his command.

he met Betty Carver, a widow with two young sons. He made himself a friend to the boys, teaching them to ski and skate, and thus was able to get to know their mother better.

## Tragedy Strikes

Montgomery and Betty Carver were married in 1927 and were rarely apart for the next ten years. Their only child, David, was born in 1928. In 1937, however, Betty was bitten on the leg by an insect while on a beach outing. The bite became infected and, although the leg was amputated, the operation came too late to save her life. Montgomery was devastated. Betty was the only person, his son included, who ever had his unconditional love. He was never known thereafter to have another romantic interest.

Later that year Montgomery was promoted to brigadier general but was increasingly unpopular among his contemporaries. "He was probably the most discussed general in the British Army before the war," one of them wrote, "and—except for those who had served under him—not a popular figure."[146] When General Archibald Wavell told a selection board he wanted Montgomery as commander of one of his divisions, other officers breathed a sigh of relief. "Everyone always agreed that he ought to be promoted," Wavell wrote, "but every other commander . . . had always excellent reasons for finding someone else more suitable than Monty."[147]

It was at the head of the Third Division that Montgomery went to France at the outbreak of World War II. The gulf between his army and the Germans soon became apparent. He wrote:

> The British Army was totally unfit to fight a first class war on the continent of Europe. . . . In the years preceding the outbreak of war no large-scale exercises with troops had been held in England for some time. Indeed the Regular Army was unfit to take part in a realistic exercise. The Field Army had an inadequate signals system, no administrative backing, and no organisation for high command. . . . The transport was inadequate and was completed on mobilisation by vehicles requisitioned from civilian firms.[148]

After he and his division were evacuated from the beaches of Dunkirk, Montgomery was put in charge of the defense of southeastern England. He was determined that his troops would be the best trained in the country. He held regular lectures, allowing precisely thirty seconds for coughing, after which coughing was prohibited. When an overweight colonel protested that he might die if forced to undergo a mandatory exercise program, Montgomery said, "Let him die. Much better to die now rather than in the midst of battle when it might be awkward to find a replacement."[149]

## Unorthodox Methods

Montgomery's methods were unorthodox, but he got results. And results were

*British troops await evacuation from the beaches of Dunkirk. Montgomery was determined to train his soldiers so that such a defeat would not be repeated.*

what was demanded when a new commander was sought for the Eighth Army in Egypt. The British, under General Claude Auchinleck, had stopped the German and Italian troops of Erwin Rommel at El Alamein in July 1942. Simply stopping Rommel, however, was not enough for British prime minister Winston Churchill. He wanted an attack and a victory. With characteristic impertinence, Montgomery arrived at the Eighth Army headquarters two days before he was to take command and, since Auchinleck was away, began issuing orders. That night, he wrote, "it was with an insubordinate smile that I fell asleep: I was issuing orders to an army someone else reckoned he commanded."[150]

The dispirited troops responded to their energetic new commander. "We all felt," wrote his longtime chief of staff, General Francis de Guingand, "that a cool and refreshing breeze had come to relieve the oppressive and stagnant atmosphere. The effect of his [first] address was electric—it was terrific! And we all went to bed that night with new hope in our hearts, and a great confidence in the future of our Army."[151]

The hoped-for offensive, however, was not forthcoming. Montgomery's natural caution took hold. He knew that Rommel's supplies were running low and that if he waited, he could build up a huge advantage in both men and weapons. By mid-October he had 164,000 men to the enemy's 100,000 and an advantage of 1,300 to 500 in tanks. Still, Rommel had won before with the odds against him, and Montgomery knew a hard battle was ahead.

## Victory at El Alamein

Rommel had established a defensive position near El Alamein. The weakest point of Rommel's line was in the south, and Montgomery did everything possible to make the Germans think he would attack there when his real intent was to strike in the north.

Montgomery's plan succeeded, thanks in part to a huge stroke of luck. Resistance was heavy and the British lost many tanks in the minefields, but Montgomery was determined to keep the pressure on Rommel's weary forces. "The tanks *will* go through,"[152] he ordered, prepared to accept heavy losses. On November 2 Montgomery ordered an all-out assault, and the Germans began their retreat two days later.

Montgomery had won a great victory, but again it was not as decisive as it might have been. The enemy was severely damaged, and a prompt, swift pursuit might have resulted in the capture of Rommel's entire army. Montgomery, however, was taking no chances. "I am not going to have out here in North Africa any failures,"[153] he told his impatient officers. As a result, the final Axis surrender in North Africa did not occur for another six months, at the cost of many Allied lives.

Most military historians, even those sympathetic to Montgomery, are critical of his lack of pursuit after the victory at El Alamein. Later Montgomery would write, "I hold the view that the leader must know what he himself wants. . . ."[154] And yet, with all his planning for the battle, he had neglected to plan the next step. Not only did he, in historian Ronald Lewin's words, "throw away the full fruits of his victory,"[155] but he also informed Rommel how to fight the remainder of the campaign. The German general would later write that he was "quite satisfied that Montgomery would never take the risk of following up boldly."[156]

The Germans were pushed ever westward and finally surrendered in May 1943. For Montgomery, it was the peak of his career. From now until the end of the war, he

*Montgomery gauges the progress of his troops at El Alamein. Although he won the battle, Montgomery's caution cost him a decisive victory and allowed Rommel's army to escape.*

would not have the luxury of independent command but would be part of the Allied team under American general Dwight Eisenhower—and teamwork and cooperation were hardly his strong points.

## Hero of Great Britain

El Alamein made it particularly difficult for Montgomery to take on a secondary role. "Monty" was on everyone's lips as a national hero. A documentary film was made and played to packed theaters. All this served to inflate Montgomery's already considerable ego.

Montgomery had irritated the American generals from the first contact in North Africa. "He left me with the feeling that I was a poor country cousin whom he had to tolerate,"[157] General Omar Bradley wrote later. And Eisenhower said, "Montgomery's the only man in either army I can't get along with."[158]

Montgomery was aware of how he was regarded, but it made little difference. There was too much at stake, he said, for him to be diplomatic:

> I know well that I am regarded by many people as being a tiresome person. I think this is very probably true. I try hard not to be tiresome; but I have seen so many mistakes made in this war, and so many disasters happen, that I am desperately anxious to try to see that we have no more; and this often means being very tiresome.[159]

## An Estate for the Taking

Montgomery was not high-handed only when dealing with fellow generals. He had little respect for either rank or station, and when he wanted something, he would do anything to obtain it.

After the fall of France in 1940, Montgomery was in command of the troops defending southeastern England. He wanted to take a brief vacation from his headquarters and instructed an aide to find him a suitable location. The aide found a large estate nearby, owned by a nobleman who was delighted at the prospect of having Montgomery as a guest.

When the aide reported back, Montgomery said that, since he wanted absolute quiet, he would take over a wing of the house and bring his own servants. The nobleman was upset but agreed since it would be for only a few days.

Montgomery, however, expanded his plans. The aide was told to go back and tell the nobleman that the general would stay for an entire month. The nobleman was outraged and refused.

When the aide reported this, Montgomery looked up the estate on a map and decided that it was in a restricted zone. As quoted in Norman Gelb's *Ike and Monty: Generals at War*, Montgomery ordered the aide: "Kick him out. We can't have him in the way of an invasion."

The nobleman was evicted, and Montgomery moved in. When he was through with the house, he had the army take it over for the rest of the war.

Given his superior attitude, it must have been galling to Montgomery when, during the conquest of Sicily, General George Patton boldly drove his American Third Army across the north of the island and entered Messina ahead of the British. Montgomery didn't make any friends during the subsequent invasion of the Italian mainland: he landed on the "toe" of the Italian boot and encountered little opposition, but American general Mark Clark was pinned down by German troops. Despite Eisenhower's plea for him to move rapidly to Clark's aid, it took Montgomery seventeen days to go three hundred miles, and even the war correspondents traveling with him moved ahead and reached Clark's headquarters a full day ahead of Montgomery.

In the middle of the Italian campaign, Montgomery was ordered to hand over command of the Eighth Army and return to Britain to work on the plan for the invasion of France. He was given a plan drawn up two years earlier by General Frederick Morgan and, with characteristic lack of tact, pronounced it impractical. "The more I examined [the plan] . . . the more I disliked it,"[160] he wrote.

## Contribution to Victory

As it happened, he was entirely correct. Montgomery drew up a new plan, one that in the end was put into place and succeeded. While Montgomery is best known for defeating Rommel in North Africa, the planning of Operation Overlord, as the invasion of France was codenamed, was probably his most important contribution to the Allied victory in World War II.

He did much in Britain besides work on the invasion plan.

He was seemingly everywhere, visiting troops and making speeches, followed everywhere by cheering crowds and newsreel cameramen. Government leaders, including Churchill, began to think he might be considering a future in politics. A joke went around London that Churchill complained to King George VI, "I'm worried about Monty. I think he's after my job."

"Thank God!" replied the king. "I thought he was after mine."[161]

Montgomery's job during the invasion of France was to command all ground forces—British and American—until an Allied line was firmly established, at which time Eisenhower would move his

*Allied reinforcements arrive on the beaches of France after the invasion. Planning Operation Overlord was one of Montgomery's greatest contributions to the war effort.*

headquarters across the English Channel and take overall command, with Montgomery and Bradley, over the respective army groups.

In the weeks after the landing on June 6, 1944, Bradley, on the west, had trouble fighting his way through the heavily defended hedgerows of Normandy. At the same time, Montgomery, on the east, was supposed to have captured the city of Caen on the first day. He was unable to do so, and the invasion was stalled.

## Slowdown in Normandy

As a frustrated Eisenhower urged him to increase his efforts, Montgomery sent back messages insisting all was well. Things, he said, were "proceeding entirely according to plan."[162] They weren't. The eastern part of the front "will burst into flames."[163] It didn't. Members of Eisenhower's staff in London grew so tired of these rosy promises that they began referring to Montgomery as "Chief Big Wind."[164]

In later years, Montgomery would maintain that Caen was not really important and that he was doing the Americans a favor by tying down so many German troops. This view was upheld by Bradley, who wrote that "Monty's primary task was to attract German troops . . . that we might more easily . . . get into position for the break-out."[165]

The breakout finally took place in late July. Eisenhower took command in September, and Montgomery almost immediately began to complain. He repeatedly urged Eisenhower to try for a quick end to the war

with "one powerful, full-blooded thrust"[166] to Berlin with himself in command.

Eisenhower tried to turn down Montgomery's plan diplomatically, but diplomacy was lost on the arrogant Montgomery, who said privately that Eisenhower "did not know Christmas from Easter."[167] When Eisenhower visited his headquarters, he argued so passionately and rudely that the normally mild Eisenhower finally said, "Steady, Monty! You can't speak to me like that. I'm your boss."[168]

Relations grew even worse after the German counteroffensive of December 1944, known as the Battle of the Bulge. Montgomery's troops fought well and performed the vital task of holding the Germans on the north side of the salient, but most of the heavy fighting was done by Patton.

Nevertheless, at a press conference, Montgomery seemed to take all the credit, despite the fact that the Americans suffered 75,000 casualties to the British 1,400. Even his British colleagues were fed up. Lord Ismay, Churchill's chief military adviser, said he wished someone would "muzzle, or better still chloroform Monty."[169] Eisenhower was ready to fire Montgomery despite the uproar it would have caused in Britain, and only a public apology by Churchill in Parliament saved him.

## Surrender in Germany

On May 4, 1945, after the Allies had swept across the Rhine River into Germany, four top German officers came to Montgomery's headquarters to discuss a surrender. When

When top German officers visited Montgomery to discuss conditions for surrender, he refused to negotiate. Troublesome to the end, Montgomery sent copies of the surrender document to Eisenhower and kept the original for himself.

they tried to make conditions, Montgomery cut them short. "No alternative,"[170] he snapped. Once the surrender document was signed, Montgomery did not send it to Eisenhower, as requested. Instead, "I sent Photostat copies. The original is in my possession and I will never part with it."[171] Even in the final moment of victory, Montgomery had to have the last word.

Montgomery was once asked who he thought were the three greatest military commanders in history. "The other two were Alexander the Great and Napoleon,"[172] he replied, not in jest. Few,

except Montgomery himself, would rank him that high. He was an exceptional strategist, as his planning for Normandy proved, but his genius was too often twisted by his own ambition and conceit. His exploits in North Africa and in France, however, have given him a permanent and prominent place in the history of World War II.

# "Old Soldiers": Their Final Years

I n 1951, in his farewell address to Congress, Douglas MacArthur said, "Old soldiers never die. They just fade away."[173] With one notable exception, that is what most of the men profiled in this book did after World War II. The war had been the summit of their careers. It had been their lives' grand adventure, and nothing else would ever equal it.

Two, of course, did not live to see the war's end. Rommel was forced by Adolf Hitler to commit suicide for taking a small part in a plot on the Nazi leader's life. Yamamoto was shot down over the Solomon Islands by an American fighter pilot.

## Von Manstein

Of those who survived, most were hailed as heroes and honored for their exploits in battle. The exception was von Manstein. After being relieved of his command by Hitler, he retired to his estate, taking no part in the war, and was eventu-

ally captured by the British in 1945 and turned over to the Soviets.

Much more so than Britain and the United States, the Soviet Union was determined to punish those who had caused so much death and destruction in their homeland. They accused von Manstein of war crimes, claiming that he had known about

*Von Manstein consults with lawyers at his trial in the Soviet Union. Convicted of war crimes, he was imprisoned until 1953.*

the mass murders committed by special Nazi units during the invasion, even though they were not under his command.

Despite a vigorous defense and even though several former Allied generals spoke up for him, von Manstein was convicted. He was imprisoned and remained there until 1953, when he was released because of poor health. He subsequently became an adviser to the West German government and died in 1973.

*Montgomery admires Churchill's medals at a reunion held after the war.*

## Montgomery

Montgomery remained in Germany, serving as commander of the British occupation forces. When Brooke retired as chief of the Imperial General Staff, Montgomery took his place but did not do very well in what was essentially a political job. Later he became deputy supreme commander of the North Atlantic Treaty Organization (NATO) and retired in 1958.

He remained as difficult as ever. His *Memoirs*, published in 1959, were highly critical of Eisenhower, who was furious. Montgomery was unapologetic. He wrote to a friend that Eisenhower "reckoned his place in history as a 'Captain of War' was secure. My book has demolished that."[174] He died in 1976 on his English estate.

## Zhukov

Zhukov, like Montgomery, remained in Germany to command the occupation forces. He was highly popular in the Soviet Union—too popular for his own good. Stalin grew jealous and in 1946 sent Zhukov to an obscure post. After Stalin's death, Zhukov regained prominence and rose to become minister of defense.

His insistence on greater independence for the army, however, brought him into conflict with Soviet leader Nikita Khrushchev and he was dismissed. He remained in obscurity until Khrushchev's death in 1964, after which he was awarded the Order of Lenin and allowed to publish his memoirs. He died in 1974.

## Nimitz

Nimitz shunned the spotlight after the war just as he had while it was being fought. At first he refused to be given a parade in his honor in Washington, D.C. He relented only because Eisenhower

*After reluctantly attending a parade held in his honor in Washington, D.C. (pictured), Nimitz went on to become chief of naval operations.*

and MacArthur had already had their parades and the navy wanted one of their own.

In 1945 he succeeded Admiral King as chief of naval operations and supervised the moving of the U.S. fleet toward the nuclear age. He retired in 1947 and lived quietly until his death in 1966.

## MacArthur

MacArthur did, indeed, fade away, but not for several years. From 1945 to 1950 he governed occupied Japan, instituting many social and governmental reforms. Soon after the outbreak of the Korean War, he was assigned to command United Nations troops. He repeatedly clashed with

President Harry Truman over the handling of the war and was relieved of command.

He was considered a hero by many in the United States, and there was a movement in 1952 to make him the Republican Party nominee for president. After the attempt failed, MacArthur accepted the board chairmanship of the Remington Rand Corporation and lived mostly in seclusion until his death in 1964.

## Eisenhower

The only top military leader to achieve even greater prominence than the war provided was Eisenhower. After fifteen months as supreme commander of NATO, during which he had the dubious pleasure of serving over Montgomery once more, he turned to politics. It was he, instead of MacArthur, who was the Republican nominee in 1952, and he easily defeated Adlai Stevenson to become the thirty-fourth president of the United States.

He was reelected in 1956 and presided over years of rising American prosperity that were nevertheless filled with tension because of the cold war with the Soviet Union and the threat of nuclear war. He retired in 1960 to his farm in Pennsylvania, where he spent most of his time writing until his death in 1969.

The world was changed forever by the events of 1939–1945. The nations of Western Europe—Great Britain, France, and

*MacArthur's disagreement with President Harry Truman over how to handle the Korean War cost him his command (above). Dwight and Mamie Eisenhower celebrate his victory in the 1952 presidential election (right).*

Germany—relinquished their long-held dominance of world affairs, and their places were taken by the United States and the Soviet Union. The time will come before too many decades have passed when all who fought in World War II will have passed from the scene. And yet, when the century is discussed, the war will remain its focal point and the men who commanded the opposing forces among its most influential leaders.

# ⭐ Notes ⭐

## Chapter 1: Rommel: "Desert Fox"

1. Quoted in Kenneth Macksey, *Rommel: Battles and Campaigns*. New York: Da Capo Press, 1997, p. 65.
2. Quoted in Desmond Young, *Rommel, the Desert Fox*. New York: Harper & Row, 1950, p. 75.
3. Quoted in Ward Rutherford, *Rommel*. London: Hamlyn Publishing Group, 1981, pp. 44–45.
4. Quoted in Young, *Rommel, the Desert Fox*, p. 48.
5. Quoted in Macksey, *Rommel*, p. 55.
6. David Fraser, *Knight's Cross*. New York: HarperCollins, 1993, p. 232.
7. Quoted in Macksey, *Rommel*, p. 57.
8. Quoted in Young, *Rommel, the Desert Fox*, p. xii.
9. Quoted in Fraser, *Knight's Cross*, p. 303.

## Chapter 2: Zhukov: Soviet Hero

10. Quoted in Otto Preston Chaney, *Zhukov*. Norman: University of Oklahoma Press, 1971, p. 38.
11. Georgi Zhukov, *Zhukov's Greatest Battles*. Translated by Theodore Shabad. New York: Harper & Row, 1969, p. 8.
12. Quoted in Chaney, *Zhukov*, p. 21.
13. Quoted in Chaney, *Zhukov*, p. 146.
14. Georgi Zhukov, *The Memoirs of Marshal Zhukov*. New York: Delacorte Press, 1971, p. 11.
15. Quoted in Zhukov, *Zhukov's Greatest Battles*, p. 5.
16. Quoted in Chaney, *Zhukov*, p. 77.
17. Zhukov, *The Memoirs of Marshal Zhukov*, p. 316.
18. Quoted in Chaney, *Zhukov*, p. 145.
19. Zhukov, *Zhukov's Greatest Battles*, p. 55.
20. Quoted in Zhukov, *The Memoirs of Marshal Zhukov*, p. 339.
21. Quoted in Zhukov, *Zhukov's Greatest Battles*, p. 132.
22. Zhukov, *Zhukov's Greatest Battles*, p. 150.
23. Quoted in Chaney, *Zhukov*, pp. 244–45.
24. Zhukov, *Zhukov's Greatest Battles*, p. 231.
25. Quoted in Chaney, *Zhukov*, p. 254.
26. Quoted in Chaney, *Zhukov*, p. 254.
27. Quoted in Otto Preston Chaney, *Zhukov: Marshal of the Soviet Union*. New York: Ballantine Books, 1974, p. 120.
28. Zhukov, *Zhukov's Greatest Battles*, p. 275.
29. Quoted in Chaney, *Zhukov*, p. 314.
30. Quoted in Zhukov, *The Memoirs of Marshal Zhukov*, p. 618.
31. Quoted in Chaney, *Zhukov: Marshal of the Soviet Union*, p. 159.

## Chapter 3: Von Manstein: Hitler's Harshest Critic

32. Erich von Manstein, *Lost Victories*. Translated and edited by Anthony G. Powell. Novato, CA: Presidio Press, 1982, p. 547.

33. Quoted in R. T. Paget, *Manstein*. London: Collins, 1951, p. 38.

34. Von Manstein, *Lost Victories*, p. 120.

35. Quoted in Paget, *Manstein*, p. 22.

36. Von Manstein, *Lost Victories*, p. 127.

37. Quoted in Lord Carver, "Manstein," in *Hitler's Generals*, edited by Correlli Barnett. New York: Quill/William Morrow, 1989, p. 228.

38. Von Manstein, *Lost Victories*, p. 175.

39. Von Manstein, *Lost Victories*, p. 185.

40. Von Manstein, *Lost Victories*, p. 203.

41. Quoted in William L. Shirer, *The Rise and Fall of the Third Reich*. New York: Simon & Schuster, 1960, p. 926.

42. Von Manstein, *Lost Victories*, p. 320.

43. Shirer, *The Rise and Fall of the Third Reich*, p. 930.

44. Von Manstein, *Lost Victories*, p. 361.

45. Von Manstein, *Lost Victories*, p. 287.

46. Basil Liddell Hart, preface, in von Manstein, *Lost Victories*, p. 15.

47. Von Manstein, *Lost Victories*, p. 362.

48. Von Manstein, *Lost Victories*, p. 453.

49. Lord Carver, "Manstein," p. 239.

50. Von Manstein, *Lost Victories*, p. 427.

51. Von Manstein, *Lost Victories*, p. 511.

52. Von Manstein, *Lost Victories*, p. 512.

53. Von Manstein, *Lost Victories*, p. 542.

54. Von Manstein, *Lost Victories*, p. 544.

55. Quoted in Lord Carver, "Manstein," p. 221.

## Chapter 4: Yamamoto: Reluctant Hero

56. Quoted in John Deane Potter, *Admiral of the Pacific*. London: William Heinemann, 1965, p. 319.

57. Quoted in Hiroyuki Agawa, *The Reluctant Admiral: Yamamoto and the Imperial Navy*. Translated by John Bester. Tokyo: Kodansha International, 1979, p. 2.

58. Quoted in Burke Davis, *Get Yamamoto*. New York: Random House, 1969, p. 27.

59. Quoted in Agawa, *The Reluctant Admiral*, p. 75.

60. Quoted in Agawa, *The Reluctant Admiral*, p. 109.

61. Quoted in Davis, *Get Yamamoto*, p. 28.

62. Quoted in Potter, *Admiral of the Pacific*, p. 31.

63. Quoted in Potter, *Admiral of the Pacific*, p. 24.

64. Quoted in Potter, *Admiral of the Pacific*, p. 35.

65. Quoted in Agawa, *The Reluctant Admiral*, p. 189.

66. Quoted in Potter, *Admiral of the Pacific*, p. 69.

67. Quoted in Davis, *Get Yamamoto*, p. 40.

68. Quoted in Potter, *Admiral of the Pacific*, p. 129.

69. Quoted in Davis, *Get Yamamoto*, p. 66.

70. Quoted in Davis, *Get Yamamoto*, p. 72.

71. Quoted in Agawa, *The Reluctant Admiral*, p. 334.

72. Quoted in Davis, *Get Yamamoto*, p. 7.

73. Quoted in Potter, *Admiral of the Pacific*, p. 307.

74. Quoted in Potter, *Admiral of the Pacific*, p. 319.

### Chapter 5: MacArthur: "I Shall Return"

75. Quoted in William Manchester, *American Caesar*. Boston: Little, Brown, 1978, p. 280.

76. Quoted in Gavin Long, *MacArthur as Military Commander*. London: B. T. Batsford, 1969, p. 4.

77. Quoted in Long, *MacArthur as Military Commander*, p. 31.

78. Quoted in Army Times editors, *The Banners and the Glory*. New York: G. P. Putnam's Sons, 1965, p. 66.

79. Quoted in Long, *MacArthur as Military Commander*, p. 74.

80. Quoted in Manchester, *American Caesar*, p. 240.

81. Quoted in Manchester, *American Caesar*, p. 238.

82. Quoted in Army Times editors, *The Banners and the Glory*, p. 104.

83. Quoted in Manchester, *American Caesar*, p. 281.

84. Quoted in Long, *MacArthur as Military Commander*, p. 115.

85. Quoted in Manchester, *American Caesar*, p. 283.

86. Quoted in Army Times editors, *The Banners and the Glory*, p. 107.

87. Quoted in Long, *MacArthur as Military Commander*, p. 147.

88. Quoted in Manchester, *American Caesar*, p. 369.

89. Quoted in Manchester, *American Caesar*, p. 389.

90. Quoted in Army Times editors, *The Banners and the Glory*, p. 119.

91. Quoted in Manchester, *American Caesar*, p. 453.

92. Quoted in Manchester, *American Caesar*, p. 352.

### Chapter 6: Nimitz: The Quiet Hero

93. Quoted in Frank A. Driskill and Dede W. Casad, *Admiral of the Hills*. Austin, TX: Eakin Press, 1983, p. 5.

94. Quoted in E. B. Potter, *Nimitz*. Norwalk, CT: Easton Press, 1976, p. 9.

95. Quoted in Potter, *Nimitz*, p. 10.

96. Quoted in Potter, *Nimitz*, p. 16.

97. Quoted in Edwin P. Hoyt, *How They Won the War in the Pacific*. New York: Weybright and Talley, 1970, p. 51.

98. Quoted in Potter, *Nimitz*, p. 21.

99. Quoted in Potter, *Nimitz*, p. 78.

100. Quoted in Driskill and Casad, *Admiral of the Hills*, p. 161.

101. Quoted in Driskill and Casad, *Admiral of the Hills*, p. 158.

102. Quoted in Potter, *Nimitz*, p. 107.

103. Quoted in Potter, *Nimitz*, p. 190.

104. Quoted in Driskill and Casad, *Admiral of the Hills*, p. 191.

105. Quoted in Hoyt, *How They Won the War in the Pacific*, p. 428.

106. Quoted in Potter, *Nimitz*, p. 344.

107. Quoted in Hoyt, *How They Won the War in the Pacific*, p. 166.

108. Quoted in Potter, *Nimitz*, p. 382.

109. Quoted in Potter, *Nimitz*, p. 390.

110. Quoted in Potter, *Nimitz*, p. 396.

111. Quoted in Potter, *Nimitz*, p. 222.

112. Quoted in Hoyt, *How They Won the War in the Pacific*, p. 504.

## Chapter 7: Eisenhower: Conqueror of Europe

113. Quoted in Alan Wykes, "Eisenhower," in *Great American Generals of World War II*. Greenwich, CT: Bison Books, 1981, p. 176.

114. Quoted in Merle Miller, *Ike the Soldier*. New York: G. P. Putnam's Sons, 1987, p. 17.

115. Dwight D. Eisenhower, *In Review*. Garden City, NY: Doubleday, 1969, p. 40.

116. Quoted in Miller, *Ike the Soldier*, p. 364.

117. Quoted in Stephen Ambrose, *The Supreme Commander*. Garden City, NY: Doubleday, 1970, p. 68.

118. Quoted in E. K. G. Sixsmith, *Eisenhower*. London: B. T. Batsford, 1973, p. 56.

119. Quoted in Ambrose, *The Supreme Commander*, p. 615.

120. Quoted in Miller, *Ike the Soldier*, p. 495.

121. Quoted in Ambrose, *The Supreme Commander*, p. 174.

122. Quoted in Wykes, "Eisenhower," p. 230.

123. Quoted in Miller, *Ike the Soldier*, p. 495.

124. Quoted in Miller, *Ike the Soldier*, p. 558.

125. Eisenhower, *In Review*, p. 59.

126. Quoted in Miller, *Ike the Soldier*, p. 495.

127. Quoted in Ambrose, *The Supreme Commander*, p. 320.

128. Quoted in Miller, *Ike the Soldier*, p. 614.

129. Quoted in Miller, *Ike the Soldier*, p. 618.

130. Quoted in Ambrose, *The Supreme Commander*, p. 435.

131. Quoted in Miller, *Ike the Soldier*, p. 663.

132. Quoted in Wykes, "Eisenhower," p. 288.

133. Quoted in Miller, *Ike the Soldier*, p. 778.

134. Sixsmith, *Eisenhower*, p. 221.

## Chapter 8: Montgomery: A Study in Contrasts

135. Quoted in Norman Gelb, *Ike and Monty: Generals at War*. New York: William Morrow, 1994, p. 329.

136. Quoted in Alun Chalfont, *Montgomery of Alamein*. New York: Atheneum, 1976, p. 1.

137. Quoted in Ronald Lewin, *Montgomery as Military Commander*. New York: Stein and Day, 1971, p. 262.

138. Quoted in Chalfont, *Montgomery of Alamein*, p. 25.

139. Quoted in Gelb, *Ike and Monty*, p. 24.

140. Quoted in Chalfont, *Montgomery of Alamein*, p. 56.

141. Quoted in Lewin, *Montgomery as Military Commander*, p. 7.

142. Quoted in Chalfont, *Montgomery of Alamein*, p. 61.

143. Quoted in Lewin, *Montgomery as Military Commander*, p. 13.

144. Quoted in Lewin, *Montgomery as Military Commander*, p. 15.

145. Quoted in Chalfont, *Montgomery as Military Commander*, p. 95.

146. Quoted in Gelb, *Ike and Monty*, p. 59.

147. Quoted in Lewin, *Montgomery as Military Commander*, p. 22.

148. Quoted in Gelb, *Ike and Monty*, p. 61.

149. Quoted in Gelb, *Ike and Monty*, p. 92.

150. Quoted in Lewin, *Montgomery as Military Commander*, p. 155.

151. Quoted in Gelb, *Ike and Monty*, p. 142.

152. Quoted in Chalfont, *Montgomery of Alamein*, p. 187.

153. Quoted in Gelb, *Ike and Monty*, p. 168.

154. Quoted in Lewin, *Montgomery as Military Commander*, p. 94.

155. Lewin, *Montgomery as Military Commander*, p. 94.

156. Quoted in Gelb, *Ike and Monty*, p. 167.

157. Quoted in Gelb, *Ike and Monty*, p. 298.

158. Quoted in Gelb, *Ike and Monty*, p. 12.

159. Quoted in Gelb, *Ike and Monty*, p. 219.

160. Quoted in R. W. Thompson, *Montgomery the Field Marshal*. New York: Charles Scribner's Sons, 1969, p. 36.

161. Quoted in Gelb, *Ike and Monty*, p. 208.

162. Quoted in Gelb, *Ike and Monty*, p. 322.

163. Quoted in Thompson, *Montgomery the Field Marshal*, p. 97.

164. Quoted in Gelb, *Ike and Monty*, p. 325.

165. Quoted in Thompson, *Montgomery the Field Marshal*, p. 100.

166. Quoted in Gelb, *Ike and Monty*, p. 348.

167. Quoted in Chalfont, *Montgomery of Alamein*, p. 257.

168. Quoted in Lewin, *Montgomery as Military Commander*, p. 235.

169. Quoted in Gelb, *Ike and Monty*, p. 398.

170. Quoted in Thompson, *Montgomery the Field Marshal*, p. 310.

171. Quoted in Chalfont, *Montgomery of Alamein*, p. 273.

172. Quoted in Chalfont, *Montgomery of Alamein*, p. 329.

## Epilogue: "Old Soldiers": Their Final Years

173. Quoted in Manchester, *American Caesar*, p. 661.

174. Quoted in Gelb, *Ike and Monty*, p. 442.

# ★ For Further Reading ★

Bruce Bliven Jr., *Story of D-Day*. New York: Random House, 1987. Anecdotes from and about generals and ordinary soldiers are sprinkled throughout this history of one of World War II's biggest battles.

Kenneth M. Deitch and JoAnne B. Weisman, *Dwight D. Eisenhower: Man of Many Hats*. Lowell, MA: Discovery Enterprises, 1990. Interesting biography follows Eisenhower's life by the various hats he wore, including football helmet, army headgear, golf cap.

Walter G. Oleksy, *Military Leaders of World War II*. New York: Facts On File, 1994. Ten American military leaders are profiled, including Nimitz, MacArthur, Eisenhower, Bradley, LeMay, and Patton.

Peter Lars Sandberg, *Dwight D. Eisenhower*. New Haven, CT: Chelsea House Publishers, 1986. Biography of Eisenhower that includes both his military and political careers.

William R. Sanford, Ron Knapp, and Carl R. Green, *American Generals of World War II*. Springfield, NJ: Enslow Publishers, 1998. Profiles of Eisenhower, MacArthur, Patton, Marshall, Matthew Ridgway, Henry Arnold, Curtis LeMay, Omar Bradley, Holland Smith, and Joseph Stillwell.

Robert Alan Scott and John Anthony Scott, *Douglas MacArthur and the Century of War*. New York: Facts On File, 1997. Biography covering the long and controversial military career of MacArthur.

# ★ Works Consulted ★

Hiroyuki Agawa, *The Reluctant Admiral: Yamamoto and the Imperial Navy*. Translated by John Bester. Tokyo: Kodansha International, 1979. Excellent biography of the Japanese navy's commander in chief written from a countryman's point of view.

Stephen Ambrose, *The Supreme Commander*. Garden City, NY: Doubleday, 1970. Biography of Eisenhower by one of the outstanding authors of World War II history. Concentrates almost entirely on the 1941–1945 period.

Army Times editors, *The Banners and the Glory*. New York: G. P. Putnam's Sons, 1965. Interesting biography of Douglas MacArthur, although slanted very much in favor of the general.

———, *The Challenge and the Triumph*. New York: G. P. Putnam's Sons, 1966. Highly favorable biography of Dwight Eisenhower that tends to avoid any controversial aspects of his career.

Lord Carver, "Manstein." In *Hitler's Generals*, edited by Correlli Barnett. New York: Quill/William Morrow, 1989. The former British field marshal's account of von Manstein's life and career is one of twenty chapters on German generals of World War II.

Alun Chalfont, *Montgomery of Alamein*. New York: Atheneum, 1976. Very well written biography of Montgomery that does not get bogged down in military details.

Otto Preston Chaney, *Zhukov*. Norman: University of Oklahoma Press, 1971. A comprehensive biography of the Soviet marshal based both on his memoirs and on recollections of those who served with and opposed him.

———, *Zhukov: Marshal of the Soviet Union*. New York: Ballantine Books, 1974. Shortened version, with some additions, of the author's much more comprehensive biography.

Burke Davis, *Get Yamamoto*. New York: Random House, 1969. Interesting account of the American plan to ambush and shoot down the airplane carrying the Japanese admiral in 1943.

Frank A. Driskill and Dede W. Casad, *Admiral of the Hills*. Austin, TX: Eakin Press, 1983. Biography of Admiral Chester Nimitz with special emphasis on his boyhood and youth in Texas.

Dwight D. Eisenhower, *In Review*. Garden City, NY: Doubleday, 1969. This pictorial autobiography combines text from Eisenhower's two earlier books, *Crusade in Europe* and *At Ease*.

David Fraser, *Knight's Cross*. New York: HarperCollins, 1993. Comprehensive biography of General Erwin Rommel that gives more space to his exploits in France than most accounts.

Norman Gelb, *Ike and Monty: Generals at War*. New York: William Morrow, 1994. Highly entertaining account of the problems between the patient Eisenhower and his difficult subordinate Montgomery.

Edwin P. Hoyt, *How They Won the War in the Pacific*. New York: Weybright and Talley, 1970. Comprehensive account of the naval war in the Pacific with special attention to the life and role of Chester Nimitz.

Ronald Lewin, *Montgomery as Military Commander*. New York: Stein and Day, 1971. Penetrating and often highly critical study of Montgomery's ability as a soldier and an assessment of his career.

Gavin Long, *MacArthur as Military Commander*. London: B. T. Batsford, 1969. Excellent biography with particular detail to Douglas MacArthur's military campaigns, complete with photographs and maps.

Kenneth Macksey, *Rommel: Battles and Campaigns*. New York: Da Capo Press, 1997. Extensive and frequently critical look at Rommel's military abilities. Great detail on campaigns in North Africa, including maps showing troop movements.

William Manchester, *American Caesar*. Boston: Little, Brown, 1978. Masterful and comprehensive biography of Douglas MacArthur that thoroughly examines both his virtues and his faults.

Erich von Manstein, *Lost Victories*. Translated and edited by Anthony G. Powell. Novato, CA: Presidio Press, 1982. The German field marshal's personal account of his campaigns during World War II. Von Manstein's accounts of his arguments with Hitler are particularly revealing.

Merle Miller, *Ike the Soldier*. New York: G. P. Putnam's Sons, 1987. Very comprehensive and highly entertaining biography of Eisenhower. Very long, but nicely organized into short chapters.

R. T. Paget, *Manstein*. London: Collins, 1951. Equal space is given to von Manstein's life and career and to his trial on charges of war crimes in this book by the British attorney who defended him.

E. B. Potter, *Nimitz*. Norwalk, CT: Easton Press, 1976. Written with the cooperation of the Nimitz family, this is the most comprehensive biography of Admiral Chester Nimitz.

John Deane Potter, *Admiral of the Pacific*. London: William Heinemann, 1965. Comprehensive biography of Japanese admiral Yamamoto Isoroku.

Ward Rutherford, *Rommel*. London: Hamlyn Publishing Group, 1981. Excellent, short biography of Rommel made even better by more than one hundred photographs.

William L. Shirer, *The Rise and Fall of the Third Reich*. New York: Simon & Schuster,

1960. Written by an award-winning journalist, this is one of the most comprehensive and readable of the histories of Nazi Germany.

E. K. G. Sixsmith, *Eisenhower*. London: B. T. Batsford, 1973. Concise analysis of Eisenhower's role as supreme Allied commander in Europe. One of a series that also includes MacArthur, Patton, Montgomery, and Stalin.

R. W. Thompson, *Montgomery the Field Marshal*. New York: Charles Scribner's Sons, 1969. Comprehensive account of Montgomery's activities from the invasion of Normandy until the surrender of Germany.

Lawrence S. Wittner, ed., *MacArthur*. Englewood Cliffs, NJ: Prentice-Hall, 1971. Collection of writings by and about Douglas MacArthur, including various evaluations of his military ability and his place in history.

Alan Wykes, "Eisenhower," in *Great American Generals of World War II*. Greenwich, CT: Bison Books, 1981. Excellent, well-illustrated biography in this large volume that also includes sections on Patton and MacArthur.

Desmond Young, *Rommel, the Desert Fox*. New York: Harper & Row, 1950. Highly entertaining and insightful biography of Rommel written by a veteran officer of the British forces that Rommel fought in North Africa.

Georgi Zhukov, *Zhukov's Greatest Battles*. Translated by Theodore Shabad. New York: Harper & Row, 1969. First-person accounts of the battles of Leningrad, Moscow, Kursk, and Berlin excerpted from Zhukov's memoirs with explanatory material from veteran reporter Harrison Salisbury.

———, *The Memoirs of Marshal Zhukov*. New York: Delacorte Press, 1971. Personal recollections of the career of the greatest of the military leaders of the Soviet Union during World War II.

# ✯ Index ✯

# ★ Picture Credits ★

Cover photo: Digital Stock
AP/Wide World Photos, 9, 17, 71, 94 (bottom)
Archive Photos, 20, 25, 27, 29, 91, 93
Brown Brothers, 11, 53, 83 (bottom), 95
Corbis, 15, 22, 30, 31, 35, 45, 56, 57, 62, 68, 76
Corbis/Hulton-Deutsch Collection, 19, 23, 39, 52, 88
Corbis/Schenectady Museum; Hall of Electrical History
    Foundation, 49
Corbis/Patrick Ward, 85
Corbis-Bettmann, 7 (top of page), 8, 21, 37, 42, 51, 54, 78, 79
Digital Stock, 5, 40, 46, 50, 61, 70, 72, 81
FPG International, 64, 74, 94 (top), 96
Library of Congress, 32, 66, 73
National Archives, 10, 12, 77
North Wind Picture Archives, 7 (top right)
pixelpartners, 7 (bottom left), 13, 41, 59, 83 (top), 89
Popperfoto/Archive Photos, 97 (bottom)
U.S. Army, courtesy Harry S Truman Library, 97 (top)

## ★ About the Author ★

William W. Lace is a native of Fort Worth, Texas. He holds a bachelor's degree from Texas Christian University, a master's from East Texas State University, and a doctorate from the University of North Texas. After working for newspapers in Baytown, Texas, and Fort Worth, he joined the University of Texas at Arlington as sports information director and later became the director of the news service. He is now executive assistant to the chancellor for the Tarrant County College District in Fort Worth. He and his wife, Laura, live in Arlington and have two children. Lace has written numerous other works for Lucent Books, one of which—*The Death Camps* in the Holocaust Library series—was selected by the New York Public Library for its 1999 Recommended Teenage Reading List.